Growing the Small Church

a guide for church leaders

C. Wayne Zunkel

Acknowledgments

My Thanks to . . .

Win Arn, who introduced me to the field of Church Growth when I was very much a skeptic.

Irven Stern, a fellow pastor, who encouraged me to give leadership in my own district in this field.

Donald McGavran, who wrote the foundational documents of the modern Church Growth movement and whose ideas have set fires burning in my brain.

The apostle Paul, who made it work centuries before and left volumes of insights.

Peter Wagner and some wonderful, thoughtful, skilled scholars and friends at Fuller. To show the kind of people they are: they invite their critics in for several days not to argue but to learn from them. They have to be the most open, hungry, teachable teachers I have ever met.

Peter Wagner and *Ray Anderson,* who encouraged me to write this book and who read the initial manuscript.

Marilyn McGinnis, who typed the manuscript and gave many valuable suggestions.

Marilyn Koehler for many of the lesson helps used after each chapter.

Lois Curley, who contacted publishers and added immeasurably to the final product.

Roger and *Alice Schrage* and *John Savage,* who contributed large chunks of insights. Special thanks to Cathy Earhart and Max Kennedy.

My parents, *Charles* and *Cleda Zunkel:* my dad was involved in church planting as a national executive for ten years; both have shepherds' hearts. They planted the concern.

The wonderful teachers in the churches I serve and irreplaceable friends from past congregations. They are the ones who have helped me "context" the principles and theories.

Published by David C. Cook Publishing Co., 850 N. Grove Ave., Elgin, IL 60120.
Printed in the United States of America.

Dedicated
   to the members of the congregations
   where I have served—
      Midland, Mich., and Reisterstown, Md.,
      Harrisburg and Elizabethtown, Pa.,
      Glendale and Panorama City, Calif.,—
   who have taught me,
      ministered to me,
        loved and nourished me,
   and given to me
      far more than I have ever given to them.

Contents

Introduction

The focus of this study together is growth for congregations with fewer than 200 members. What we will look at grows out of reading, classes, and nationwide workshops. But most of all, it grows out of real-life experience: the successes and failures that have come as Church Growth principles have been applied in difficult, actual settings.

A ministerial friend asked, "If the churches you serve fail to grow after you have talked so much about growth, won't that discredit what you say?" My response was that it will be a reflection on me and the churches I serve, not on the principles of Church Growth.

We know the things that make for growth.

I go to a doctor. He tells me I have high blood pressure. He tells me not to use salt and to begin taking a small pill daily. Because the pill removes sodium and potassium from the body, I am to eat a banana a day to replace the potassium. If I don't do what he says, continuing high blood pressure is not his fault nor the fault of medical science.

The truth is, *your church can grow* (1) if it *wants* to grow; (2) if it is willing to apply growth principles; (3) if it is willing to pay the price of growth; and (4) provided it does not have a terminal illness.

George Hunter of the United Methodist Church says that in his denomination enough research has been conducted and enough on-site experience has been gained to show growth in every one of its target churches, large and small in various kinds of settings.

An extensive United Church of Christ study of small churches, which we will explore later, concluded that any church can grow when it *decides* to. One review of the report is entitled, "Small by Design."[1]

Dean Kelley has a book, *Why Conservative Churches Are Growing,* which he says was misnamed by the publishers. He says it should have been named, "Why churches that make demands are growing." He argues that *strict* churches are strong, and that strong churches grow. Surveying the denominations that have lost large numbers of people in recent years, he writes:

The process we see at work in the churches is *probably not reversible.* Having once succumbed to weakness, a church is unlikely to recover, not because measures leading to recovery could not be prescribed and instituted . . . but because the persons who now occupy positions of leadership and followership in the church will not find them congenial and will not want to institute them. They prefer a church which is not too strenuous or demanding—a church, in fact, which is dying.[2]

Turnaround is difficult. But we *know* the things that make for growth. The problem in this area, as in every other area in our lives, is that *knowing* and *doing* are not the same. The key lies with us. And with the power of God.

This is more than a book to be read and understood. It is a tool to be used with a congregation. It is meant to be studied, discussed, assimilated.

If this is to be used in a group, it is essential that the leadership of the church be involved: the pastor, members of the governing board, the informal decision makers, church school teachers, music personnel, and as many members as possible.

A climate needs to be set, a time established for holding the sessions, class members recruited.

At the end of each chapter are suggestions for use: studies to be conducted, personal inventories to be taken, graphs and charts to be filled out. Any of these forms may be reproduced as handouts without obtaining reprint permission.

For best involvement, each member of the class should be encouraged to have a copy of this book and read each chapter before the session. Second best is to have several copies and assign the presentation of various sections of each chapter to class members. The more who come to a class session with this background, the richer will be your time together.

A list of things to do before the classes start will

come first after each chapter. Diagrams for overhead transparencies and "medical examination" sheets are often included: Transparencies can be made straight from the book on most photocopiers or at quick-print shops. If your church does not own an overhead projector, sometimes one can be borrowed from a school. If students do not have their own books, medical examination sheets need to be reproduced for each student.*

All of the films suggested are excellent portrayals of the truth in that chapter. They are well done, interesting, and often filled with humor.

Films should be ordered *now*.

Institute for American Church Growth
709 E. Colorado Blvd., #150
Pasadena, CA 91101
Call 24 hours toll-free 800-423-4844

Films you will need:

First week: *And They Said It Couldn't Be Done!* (30 min.) A stirring story of faith attempting impossible things.

Second week: *The Sacrifice* (10 min.) A father's difficult choice between the life of his son and the lives of a trainload of people.

Tenth Week: *Discover Your Gifts* (30 min.) A layman's struggle to discover his gifts. Humor, insight.

Eleventh week: *But I'm Just a Layman* (26 min.) The same layman struggles with his assumption that evangelism is the pastor's job.

Congregation Meeting on Growth, or Growth Banquet: *The Great Commission Sunday School* (27 min.) The same layman tries to discover why their church school is not as strong as it once was. Humorous, helpful.

A secretary should be appointed to take notes of suggestions and decisions for action as you go along. If no one records these, they will be lost.

Equipment needed:
a kitchen timer with bell
overhead projector (available from a
school if you do not own one)
16 millimeter movie projector
screen (as large as possible)
two projection tables (one for overheads
and one for movies)
extension cords
chalkboard
extra pencils
extra paper

Participants may be asked to bring their own Bibles each week (whatever version they prefer), pencils, and perhaps a notebook to log their ideas.

If you read this book alone and never intend to use it as material for a class, the exercises are still worth doing on your own. They can help *you*, at least, better understand your congregation's strengths and weaknesses and its mission.

---

* If you wish, transparencies included in this manual are available in color through Charles E. Fuller Theological Institute of Evangelism and Church Growth, P.O. Box 989, Pasadena, CA 91102. (213) 449-0425.

1. Theodore H. Erickson, *Small by Design,* Consultation on the Small Church, Lancaster Theological Seminary, April 26, 1977.

2. Dean M. Kelley, "Preface to the First Edition," *Why Conservative Churches Are Growing* (New York: Harper and Row, 1972), pp. xvii-xviii.

1 Small Is Not Ugly

Most of the examples of church growth in the United States are the giants. I sat in an excellent seminar listening to one of the top men in the field setting forth bedrock principles. The minister sitting next to me whispered with anger and discouragement, "There he goes again, talking about large churches."

Basic Principles Refocused

But the superchurches started small. Pastor Robert Schuller[1] talks movingly of his experience in faith, coming to Southern California with only a list of possible places where a new church might meet. Among them was a Seventh-Day Adventist church, a funeral parlor chapel, a school auditorium, and a lodge hall. *Last* on his list was a drive-in theater.

But that's where he began, preaching from the sticky tar paper roof of the projection booth. He and his wife used a $300 parting gift from their last parish and borrowed against their insurance policies to rent a trailer and make a down payment on a two-manual electronic organ. His majestic Crystal Cathedral today seems worlds removed from the scene of faith and struggle a few short years before.

Jack Hayford began with a small, plateaued Foursquare church. Nine people attended his first meeting. It was not until, in utter discouragement, he humbled himself, promising to be pastor of a small church *the rest of his life* if that was what God wanted, that growth came to the now huge Church on the Way in Van Nuys, California.

The lessons we will explore together in this book grow out of the same growth principles used by the giants. But here they are applied to small, struggling churches.

John Wimber, a Church Growth consultant, says the average congregation in the United States has fewer than 200 members. The average-sized Sunday morning worship is 65. Nearly one out of five congregations in the United States averages between 20 and 40 at worship.[2]

Where do such churches begin? What hope is there for the mass of "average" congregations? Less than 500 churches in our entire nation have an average Sunday morning attendance of more than 1,000. What most of us need is not the story of their success but baby steps we can begin to take here and now.

The Problem of Morale

During college and seminary I had served small summer pastorates. But upon entering the full-time ministry, the first two churches I served were larger, active churches with multiple staff. Imagine the shock to me when I then took two small churches in Southern California. Both had lost many members. In a twelve-year period beginning in the 1960's, one had lost 58 percent of its membership, the other 85 percent. That second one greeted me with 12 to 15 persons on a Sunday morning, less than half the size of the choir in the previous church I had served. I later learned that most of them had agreed to "try it" for just one more year.

In such a setting, the first task was not growth but "bottoming out," plugging the holes in a rapidly sinking ship. There was no Sunday school, no choir, a handful of people on what remained of a church board.

The immediate problem was morale. A will to go on. A program attractive enough that they would want to stick with, much less begin to invite others to. The church building was in bad repair. On Monday mornings, another layman and I spent hours painting, much as a priest would set about to repair a broken-down mission in the desert. Starting new would have been easier.

One advantage for me has been that I have served a yoked parish: two small congregations with separate programs and boards join in paying my salary while I divide my time between them. This has given me a perspective I never had before in my ministry. Always before, when things went well, I took the credit. When discouraging periods came, I also took the blame.

Almost providentially, in this yoked situation when one church has gone through a discouraging period, the other has shown signs of exciting life.

Then they seem to switch, the other taking off while the first seems to regress. I bring the same sermons to both, and, hopefully, the same enthusiasm and dedication. Yet one moves while the other seems to sit.

I talked with a man who served many years as pastor to four small churches in Canada. He commented that he would have quit sooner, but every time he thought about leaving, something exciting began to happen in another of the four.

There is ebb and flow in the life of any congregation. In a small congregation, the ebb can be devastating. It takes great faith and a masterful dose of patience—the kind of patience that is a fruit of the Spirit of God Himself—to know that things will begin to move again.

"Management by Objectives," "Management by Results," and even "Management by Crisis" are familiar terms. But a new phrase—"Management by Rescue" or "Turnaround Management"—is now beginning to be used. The subject cannot be found in the curriculum of any of our colleges or business schools, nor does it appear in credit and loan manuals. But it is beginning to be successfully practiced.[3]

As we develop growth principles for small churches, we will relate also principles from Turnaround Management when they apply.

The Thirty-Year Cycle

John Wimber, who as a church consultant visited more than 600 congregations of many denominations across the United States,[4] indicates that most congregations go through a thirty-year pattern of growth. Their membership pattern shows early growth, a leveling off, and a slow decline. After thirty years, most congregations do not grow.

Many factors cause many congregations after age 15 to stop growing. Wimber puts it in personal terms: "I'm 46 years old. It's like my wife said, 'Let's start a family.' "

Many churches feel, "We built our sanctuary. We put forth energy and sacrificed in many ways. We're tired. We've done our part. We want to rest now. We don't care if there are a lot of people out there."

One of the principles of Turnaround Management applies at this point. Myles Ketchum, writing one of the pioneer articles in the field,[5] says that great tact is required in helping a bank or a firm (or a church!) turn around. "Nothing is gained by dwelling on the

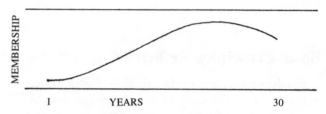

circumstances or events which contributed to the existing conditions." The approach must be "positive and forward looking." Just as Jesus approached each person not only in terms of what he had been but also what he could become, so we must approach the congregation with love, appreciation, encouragement, and great sensitivity.

Rescue Management suggests using a brief outline of previously *successful* engagements to encourage the client and to suggest the kind of result that may be expected.

We will develop this more later as we explore some of the tensions that arise as a church begins to grow.

The Riches of Small Churches

Carl S. Dudley, in his excellent book *Making the Small Church Effective,* has a simple but meaningful exercise before each chapter to help the congregation come to know itself and better appreciate itself. There is a lot to be loved and treasured in most small churches. Dudley helps to uncover that, to chart relationships, to recall the past, to understand the factors at work.[6]

Small is not ugly. Paul in his letters refers to churches that met in homes.[7] They could not have been large. Those ancient Oriental homes limited the size. Paul Minear in his book on Romans observes that evidence points to the existence of many congregations meeting in various homes scattered across Rome.[8]

In many, many small churches there is a great beauty, a rich history of great devotion, invaluable memories, and a golden record of amazing sacrifice and tenacity across many years. They are treasure chests of much good. Many have survived an inordinate amount of terrible preaching.

A tiny Church of the Brethren located in a racially turbulent city, less than half a block from the Hell's Angels motorcycle gang headquarters, had the following in its church newsletter a few years back:

> In a big world,
> the small church has remained intimate.
> In a fast world,
> the small church has been steady.
> In an expensive world,
> the small church has remained plain.
> In a complex world,
> the small church has remained simple.
> In a rational world,
> the small church has kept feeling.
> In a mobile world,
> the small church has been an anchor.
> In an anonymous world,
> the small church calls us by name.

Church bureaucrats have tried to close them down or merge them, often without success. Church planners have predicted their demise. But they live on.

Love—The Change Agent

I enjoy the story of the businessman who read a little book entitled *Men of God*. He was so moved that he determined to secure copies for all of his employees. He wired the publisher in Chicago: "Send 125 copies of *Men of God*."

The publisher wired back, "Chicago is out of *Men of God*, try Los Angeles."

Try Springfield. Try Danville. Try Pleasant Grove.

"Bloom where you are planted" is the motto we must come to understand.

If the grass is greener on the other side, it probably means your neighbor has been hard at work in his yard. Find meaning and joy where you are, or you are not likely to find it at all. All that God would do anywhere, He would begin to do in the church and setting in which you find yourself.

As you approach your small church and seek to have it grow, *love it!* Know that it will also take anger and patience and prodding and the power of God undergirding and leading all the way. But know deep in your heart that *only love* can help it grow.

Teaching Helps for Chapter 1

Before the class session:

☐ Have someone prepare an overall membership church school worship chart for your congregation similar to the one on page 2.

☐ Prepare the "In a Big World . . ." overhead.

☐ Prepare copies of Medical Chart 1, one for each student.

☐ Secure the film *And They Said It Couldn't Be Done.*

Suggested Lesson Plan

(Use as much as you have time for.)

1. If students have not read the text, present in your own words the material "Basic Principles Refocused."

2. Have students name three items that they have observed in which the small size has been a source of wonder in operation or beauty. (Possible answers: the inner ear, a blown glass object, a program chip for a computer.)

3. Name three things (other than animal or plant) that must start small but have within them the power to grow. (Yeast, dough, the human mind, a new pond.)

4. Present or review material on "The Problem of Morale." Discuss: "What factors have you noticed about a group, church, or company that you think facilitate growth?" (Clear objectives; good leadership; understandable goals; gearing up for an event/project/product to sell; belief that the product/goal is one that will enrich the lives of people; etc.)

5. Discuss: "If you were to start a new company or group to produce a product or activity for your community, how would you organize the leadership and make the workers or members an active part?"

6. Present the material on "The Riches of Small Churches." Use the overhead transparency "In a Big World . . ." at the appropriate time.

7. Have each person spend *two minutes* on column 1 of Medical Chart 1. Use a kitchen timer.

8. Then have each person fill in the dates on columns 2 and 3. Ask each person to spend *three minutes* filling in successes. Use the kitchen timer.

9. Next, ask each person, working alone, to list in column 4 some of the present strengths and past successes *on which the church might build*. What are the things you as a church have going for you? Give each person *two minutes*.

10. Share your listings, beginning first by collecting the strengths onto a chalkboard; second, share the successes experienced; finally, list those on which you might build. What do you feel good about? What do you have to build on?

Do not act on these, however, until you have a chance to check them against the things that make for growth (chapter 4).

11. Look together at the overall chart of your congregation's membership, church school, and worship.

12. Ask each student to rate his own feelings about the congregation at this time; draw this continuum on the chalkboard.

---

discouraged   tired   satisfied   hopeful   excited

Place a mental X on the line at the spot that describes your feeling.

13. Show the film: *And They Said It Couldn't Be Done.* It shares examples of faith overcoming impossible odds in Bible times and now.

14. Present the material in "Love—The Change Agent."

15. Ask everyone in the group to write a note to someone who has an admirable quality. Collect the notes, and distribute them to each person before the next session. This is your small beginning to affirm the life in your church.

16. Read together Matthew 13:31, 32. Note the words "the smallest of all seeds, but when it grows . . . the biggest of all plants."

17. Offer individual prayers about your dreams for God's church in your place.

1. Robert Schuller, *Your Church Has Real Possibilities* (Glendale, Calif.: Regal Books, 1975).
2. See also Lyle E. Schaller, *The Multiple Staff and The Larger Church* (Nashville: Abingdon, 1980), introduction.
3. John M. Durkee and Ian B. Sharlit, "Ever Try 'Management by Rescue' for Ailing Borrower?" *American Banking Journal,* March 1980, pp. 66-68. Miles K. Ketchum, "Rescue Management—A New Solution to an Old Problem," *The Journal of Commercial Banking and Lending,* December 1980, pp. 21-30.
4. John Wimber, now founding pastor of Calvary Chapel, Yorba Linda, Calif., was founder of the Fuller Evangelistic Association's Department of Church Growth.
5. Ketchum, "Rescue Management . . ." p. 26.
6. Carl Dudley, *Making the Small Church Effective* (Nashville: Abingdon, 1978).
7. Acts 20:20; Romans 16:5; I Corinthians 16:19; Colossians 4:15.
8. Paul Minear, *The Obedience of Faith: The Purposes of Paul in the Epistle to the Romans* (Naperville, Ill.: A. R. Allenson, 1971), p. ix.

Medical Chart 1—The Patient's Health

1
Our strengths NOW:

Today's date:

Now

2
Successes experienced over the past six months:

Date six months ago:

Immediate past six months

3
Successes of the past two years:

Date two years ago:

Past two years

4
FOR THE FUTURE: Present strengths and past successes on which we might build:

In a big world, the small church has remained intimate.

In a fast world, the small church has been steady.

In an expensive world, the small church has remained plain.

In a complex world, the small church has remained simple.

In a rational world, the small church has kept feeling.

In a mobile world, the small church has been an anchor.

In an anonymous world, the small church calls us by name.

2 The Natural Thing to Do

We have almost convinced ourselves that small and ingrown is the natural way for a church to be. That growing churches are mutations. Freaks. The odd ones in God's scheme of things.

We forget that growth is the natural condition in God's world. *To live is to grow.* And whether it applies to trees or turnips, tulips or tadpoles, children or churches, when you stop growing, you're through. When growth stops, death has already set in.

Growing is the natural thing to do. And a normal, healthy, loving church, set in a reasonably normal setting, grows! Naturally!

Loving people reach out in love to share that love. Excited people naturally share their excitement. If faith has meaning, *it will be shared*—as naturally as we talk about anything else that has meaning for us.

To put it negatively, you know a sickness has set in when a people have been entrusted with *the most important news of all time* and simply sit on it.

If a living faith is ours, we will find ways to pass it on.

Sharing Half a Christ?

Some suspect that when the phrase *Church Growth* is used, people really have in mind a set of sociological principles that are very far removed from the Biblical faith they want as a base.

But the truth is that the undergirding is there. The uneasiness about Church Growth comes not because *it* is not built on a solid foundation, but because *we* have moved from that foundation toward other worthy but secondary goals.

My own life was caught up in the challenge of the 1960's. In Harrisburg, Penn., another white minister, a black minister and I went to visit business leaders of our community. At that time blacks could not be meter readers for the electric or gas companies, even in black areas. They could not work at checkout counters in supermarkets in black communities or as tellers in banks. Mature men with college degrees were forced to work for the minimum wage as bellhops in hotels—only because they were black. If I had it to do over, I would again take my lumps to bear witness to the justice on which a solid Biblical faith insists.

It was easy in those drama-filled days to lose sight of the call to "make disciples," not only to witness to society, but to witness at the same time to lost and hurting individuals. Sorokin said that if there is to be change without serious disruption, we must work simultaneously at three levels—the personal, the social, and the cultural. All three must change together. This is evident throughout Scripture, within the limits allowed by the society in which they found themselves.

Christians have wrongly tried to divide themselves into two groups—those who advocate a *personal* Gospel and those who advocate a *social* Gospel. For Jesus, the two were one. One Gospel—at the same time both social and personal. He viewed the total person—body, mind, and spirit. And He ministered to the whole person in all relationships.

The poet Swinburne said, "For tender minds they served up half a Christ." The Christ God sent loved the world! And whatever destroyed people, twisted human personality, or hurt God's children, He opposed.

Amid the turmoil of the sixties, some churchmen tried to divide the Gospel. Racism and war and injustice were moved to the top of the priority list. And the caring, personal Christ, the Savior of aching hearts and lost souls, was at times forgotten.

Barrenness Theology

We had almost a *barrenness theology*. A moral relativism developed: "Whatever anyone thinks, is right for him." It may have been in response to a previous rigidity and judgmental spirit. But it came out almost like a doctor telling a patient with a broken arm, "That's all right. I love people with broken arms. You go right on, knowing that we all love you and approve of your condition."

The attempt in some circles was to say that *everything is relative*. Most people still had their own lists of rigidities, however, which in their eyes were above reproach.

We came to view the church as optional. Was it

really needed? Maybe the world would be better off with fewer churches, fewer people who call themselves Christian, some argued.

There seemed to be *almost no awareness that people are lost,* alone, afraid, hurting, dying. The Cause was the thing. The great aching of individual human hearts was sometimes not even recognized.

Meeting physical needs was felt to be enough.

There was *pessimism concerning mission* coupled with *overoptimism about the condition of people*.

For some pastors, the turnaround began when Karl Menninger, who had spent all his life in the field of psychology, wrote a book that raised the unheard-of question (in some circles) *Whatever Became of Sin?*[2]

THE FAR SIDE By GARY LARSON

© Chronicle Features, 1981 1-13

Come out of that cave and meet your doom, you miserable dragon! You can't hide in there forever, you overgrown chameleon!

Because we underestimated the presence and power of sin to shatter human lives, we also had a low and utterly inadequate view of the tremendous power of God to transform and make lives whole again.

We underestimated our own need and the need of others around us, and therefore failed to comprehend the need of us all for God.

The Church: God's Vehicle

We came to view the church as simply another human institution, and not a very good one at that. It was a church made up of hypocrites and racists and people bathed by the acids of a corrupt culture, not baptized by the rivers of God's justice.

Even today I hear people who do not realize that although the church is made up of humans who are imperfect, and thus *it* is imperfect, the church is still God's vehicle to accomplish His will in His world.

Albert Einstein, a Jew in Hitler's Germany, wrote that when Hitler came to power,

> being a lover of freedom . . . I looked to the universities to defend that freedom.
> . . . But no, the universities immediately grew silent. Then I looked to the editors of the great newspapers. . . . But they, like the universities, grew silent in a few short weeks. *Only the church* stood squarely across the path of (the) campaign for suppressing the truth. I never had any special interest in the church before. But now I feel a great affection and admiration because the church *alone* had the courage and persistence to stand for intellectual truth and moral freedom. I am forced thus to confess that what I once despised, I now praise unreservedly.

The church—not a service club or lodge, not a voluntary agency promoting this good cause or that, not a government agency—*the church* is *God's vehicle for achieving His will in His world* as no other group can.

In Poland, across years of harsh Soviet domination, it is the church that has given the heroic Poles the courage and cohesiveness to stand as no other

Eastern-bloc country has dared to stand.

My daughter keeps handing me liberation theology books and materials written by church leaders in Latin America. For centuries it seemed church leadership there was on the side of riches, domination, and corruption. But today the best hope for permanent change toward a more human society in Latin America lies with church men and women in high positions and low, empowered by the Gospel and held together by the church, willing to risk everything for dignity and freedom and basic human justice.[3]

Around the world that is true.

Some object to Church Growth as if it were putting the emphasis on a small, frail, undeserving human institution. They are the ones who have moved from the firm Biblical foundation. Have we forgotten Christ's intent that upon the Rock He will found His Church, and the gates of hell itself shall not prevail against it?

The church is imperfect because we are imperfect. But God is working in it and through it—as He works nowhere else—to accomplish His will.

Church Growth Documents You Already Own

You may not even realize it, but you already own the most important set of Church Growth documents. You may think you have not acquired a Church Growth library at this point, but you have had the basic documents all along. Your New Testament was written by missionaries to missionaries. The Gospels, the Book of Acts, the Letters were written from Church Growth people to Church Growth people about Church Growth.[4]

Before I began to study modern Church Growth understandings, our congregations engaged in a study across many weeks of the Book of Acts. We traced Paul's journeys. We derived many lessons for our own lives. For me, personally, it was a rich, thrilling experience.

But after some Church Growth studies, Acts opened up in a way I had never seen it before. I found

it bubbling with insights and strategies—some of which we will explore shortly.

It was as though I had never really read or understood the book before. It took on a whole different character with Church Growth eyes.

Everything we will explore has parallels in the early church. That's why we refer to the current studies as the *modern* Church Growth movement. The movement is not new. It is very old—as old as our Lord and the way He moved among people. As old as the first-century church.

In his studies in the 1930's, Donald McGavran found contradictory reasons given for growth or decline. Some churches said, "We're growing because we preach the true Word of God." But he also found stagnated churches saying, "We're not growing because we preach the true Word of God."

The first-century church preached the true Word of God. They were as near to the Source as any could be. And they faced impossible odds—an oppressive, unsympathetic government, nervous about this new, upsetting, subversive religion. They were small. They were scattered. They were powerless. For the most part they were terribly poor and had little formal education. They faced a vast mixture of cultures and religions. The world was big, cruel, antagonistic.

But they grew. Joyously. Naturally. Excitingly. Rapidly.

It was not studied with them. It was as natural as you please. Not easy. Not without pain or sacrifice. But it came, and got bigger and bigger, and there was no stopping it.

It just may be that they have some things to teach us.

So with your own well-worn Testament firmly in hand, come with me on an exciting journey that will reveal the keys to unlock the growth God intends.

Teaching Helps for Chapter 2

Before the class session:

☐ Secure figures for the number of people lost from your congregation (through death, transfer of membership, or inactivity) each year for the past five years. What percentage of the total membership do they represent for each of those years?

☐ Prepare the following overhead transparencies: "Barrenness Theology" and "You already own . . ."

☐ Secure the film *The Sacrifice*–a powerful movie. Not for young children.

Suggested Lesson Plan:

1. Present or review the first section of the chapter.

2. Growth as a "natural thing" contradicts some of our adult values. For example, we diet, we join groups (lodges, bridge clubs, etc.) in which the number of members is limited. Ask the following:

"In many instances we view groups in terms of what they can do *for us*. We are not so concerned about group growth as much as personal benefit. List five things your church group can do for your unchurched friend or neighbor.

"Now, thinking of that friend or neighbor, list the qualities or contributions he or she could add to the life of your church group."

3. Analyze together: "What percent of our membership do we lose each year? How many new members must we bring in just to stay even?" Use the statistics you gathered in advance.

4. Present the material on "Sharing half a Christ?" Discuss one or two questions at a time:

"How important is our faith? Can people take it or leave it alone? What happens when vast numbers of people lapse into unbelief and indifference?

"If all churches in our community were closed, would it matter?"

"Many cities are a jungle: life is not valued, there is senseless murder, little children are mutilated. Can we survive without God? Maybe the first generation would have a residue of moral values. What about the second and third?"

5. Present the material on "Barrenness Theology," using the related transparency. Discuss: "Have any of these views been a part of our thinking?"

6. Present the sections "The Church: God's Vehicle" and "Church Growth Materials You Already Own," using the transparency "You already own . . ."

7. Ask each person to list the Church Growth documents (Acts—Jude) that he or she has read in the last six months.

8. Show the film *The Sacrifice,* the story of a father who must choose between the life of his young son and a train full of people who face death. A disturbing, powerful presentation on the theme "God so loved the world that He gave His Son. . . ."

Following the film, allow two minutes for quiet reflection. Use the timer. Provide papers and pencils, and invite students to write some of their thoughts.

Then discuss what you feel the message is. Allow three minutes. Use the timer.

9. Ask: "If God paid such a price for the world, how do we excuse our indifference?"

10. Ask each person to write a few sentences on the theme "My Faith in the Church" or "What the Church Means to Me."

Let volunteers share what they have written.

11. Read together Matthew 16:12-20. What does this say to your group?

1. Eddie Gibbs, *Body Building Exercise for the Local Church* (London: Falcon, 1979), p. 13.
2. Karl Menninger, *Whatever Became of Sin?* (New York: Hawthorn, 1973).
3. See, for example, José Miguez Bonino, *Doing Theology in a Revolutionary Situation* (Philadelphia: Fortress, 1975).
4. Donald A. McGavran and Winfield C. Arn, *Ten Steps for Church Growth* (San Francisco: Harper and Row, 1977), p. 24.

BARRENNESS THEOLOGY

- *Moral relativism— whatever anyone thinks is right for him.*
- *The church is optional.*
- *No awareness that people are lost, alone, afraid, hurting, dying.*
- *Meeting physical needs is enough.*
- *Pessimistic concerning mission and overly optimistic about condition of people.*

You already own the most important set of Church Growth Documents

- *Written by church growth people to church growth people*

- *Bubbling with insights and strategies*

3 Some Assumptions

In every class I have ever taken, I have always been suspicious of a professor who pretends to be without bias. The classes I have found most helpful are those where, for example, a political science professor may say, "I am a moderate Republican. I voted for Nixon, Ford, and Reagan. These are some of my biases so you may be aware of them as I present my material."

The following are some of the assumptions I make.

Assumption 1: Our Christian faith is the most important thing we have to share.

Donald McGavran, in his book, *Understanding Church Growth,* wrote about the challenge we face:

> As in the light of Christ we look at the world—its exploding knowledge, peoples, revolutions, physical needs, desperate spiritual hunger and nakedness, and enslavement to false gods and demonic ideologies—we realize that Christian mission must certainly engage in many labors. A multitude of excellent enterprises lie around us. So great is the number and so urgent the calls, that Christians can easily lose their way among them, seeing them all equally as mission. But in doing good, they can fail of the best. In winning the preliminaries, they can lose the main game. They can be treating a troublesome itch, while the patient dies of cholera.[1]

People need bread . . . justice . . . peace. Make no mistake about that. Our Lord gave large blocks of time to meeting the physical needs of the poor and oppressed who crowded around Him.

One of the thrilling signs of our times is to see denominations and congregations labeled "evangelical" reaching out so dramatically to meet basic human need. Robert Schuller is criticized by those who feel the money spent on the Crystal Cathedral should have been spent on the poor. Schuller's response to a radio interviewer was that their offering on the day of dedication totaled $100,000 and it all went toward a new hospital in southern Mexico. With its treatment center it would serve 100,000 families. Projections are to raise nearly two million dollars during the next four years for needy causes. Schuller sees the church as providing a base for reaching out to hurting people around the world.[2]

Jesus '80, in one concert in Anaheim Stadium on May 17, 1980, raised $250,000 for Cambodian refugees.

Christians of all persuasions are coming to recognize that people need bread . . . justice . . . peace.

But even more, they need solid ground on which to stand, a strong faith around which to orient their lives.

The first church I served, in inner-city Harrisburg, Pennsylvania, was surrounded by multiproblem families. There were many fatherless homes, much unemployment, many people with little education, much alcoholism, and poor diets—children living on potato chips and Cokes. Some babies died of malnutrition.

We developed a full community program: after-school scrap crafts for young children; a basketball league for teenage boys, using a large Presbyterian church gym nearby; cooking classes and sewing classes for young mothers; a study hall and tutoring program; a civic association; a home for young women who moved to the city; a day-care center; a well-baby clinic; and on and on. But very soon I came to realize that if that was all we did, we were simply making middle-class pagans out of lower-class pagans. People needed more if their lives were to be reoriented and full.

If the Scriptures say anything, it is this: *People can survive all manner of physical hardships if they have faith.* They can manage hunger, prison, oppressive governments, sickness, loss of goods and family, even the prospect of the loss of life itself. Martin Luther could sing, "Let goods and kindred go, this mortal life also. The body they may kill; God's truth abideth still. His kingdom is forever."

And the Scriptures address the other side of that. *Physical well-being without faith is disastrous.*

13

"What does it profit," Jesus asked, "if you gain the whole world and lose your own soul?"

Marilyn Koehler, an evangelism counselor in Iowa, put it in these terms:

> We have offered
> Peace . . . without the Peacemaker
> Service . . . without the Servant
> Knowledge . . . without the Mind of Christ
> Equality, liberation, respectability . . . without the cross as a leveling experience
> Fellowship and ecumenicity . . . without knowing Christ as brother and God as Father.

Too often we have shared half a loaf or a crust of bread when people hungered for the whole Bread of life, a cup of cold water when they thirsted even more for that Spring that never runs dry.

Assumption 2: Evangelism is more than "seeking."

It is not enough to beam radio broadcasts or to plaster billboards or to distribute bumper stickers.

It is not enough to open doors of the church and announce that, of course, all people are welcome.

It is not enough to open our hearts as hurting people come to us.

It is not enough for the shepherd to stand at the gate of the fold and call to the lost sheep out on the hillside. God wants more than kindly messages or powdered milk sent to the son in the far country. He is not happy until He sees that son or daughter walking back into the home once again.[3]

An Anglican publication said it so well:
Christ is not pleased with . . .
- Fishing without catching. (Lk. 5:4-11)
- Empty banquet tables. (Lk. 14:15-23)
- Sowing without reaping. (Mt. 13:3-9)
- A fig tree that bears no fruit. (Lk. 13:6-9)
- Lost sheep that are not brought into the fold. (Mt. 18:11-14)
- A lost coin that is sought but not found. (Lk. 15:8-10)
- Harvests that are not reaped. (Mt. 9:36-38)
- Proclamation without response. (Mt. 10:14)
- Sons and daughters outside the Father's house. (Lk. 15:11-32)

Evangelism, New Testament style, is satisfied with nothing less than finding the hurt, the lonely, the lost.

Assumption 3: Numbers matter.

A census taker in the hills of West Virginia knocked at a door and asked the woman of the house how many lived there. She replied, "Well, there's Willie, and there's Sarah Jane, and there's Butch, and there's Alfred. . . ."

"No, no, no," interrupted the census taker. "Not the names, just the number."

"Mister," said the lady, rising to her full five feet, two inches, "in this house we don't have numbers. We all have names."

Every number has a name.

A woman was visiting a psychiatrist. He had established that she was married and had several children. Almost in passing he asked which of the children she loved the most. She replied that she loved them all the same.

Her answer seemed too glib. He decided to press her. "Come now," he said, "nobody loves all of their children the same."

She insisted it was true.

He decided to press some more. "Look, lady, if you won't be honest with me and level with me, you are wasting your time and mine."

She burst into tears and cried a little. Then, pulling herself together, she said, "All right. When one of my children is hurt, I love that child the most. When one of my children is sick, I love that child the most. When one of my children is bad—I don't mean naughty, I mean really bad—I love that child the most. But aside from that, I love them all the same."

Augustine said, "God loves each of us as if there were only one of us."

Numbers matter. Because each number represents a child of God.

McGavran tells of a missionary who refused to

submit numbers of converts on his report forms to the home office because he was not interested in numbers. But at the bottom he carefully detailed the number of goats, mules, chickens, and pets.

Numbers matter.

Turnaround Management, which we referred to earlier, suggests that a beginning point in any turnaround operation is a "line-by-line, item-by-item analysis."[4]

Carl George, a Church Growth consultant, tells how in the early days of his ministry he served on a staff of several people in a large church. Every Monday morning was spent in what, at the time, he regarded as a totally wasteful exercise. These highly trained persons, with salaries of professionals, some fresh from seminary and obviously (by their own admission) "terribly bright and talented," were gathered into the church office to stand around for the entire Monday morning, counting the offerings of the various church school classes and tallying the records of attendance. Only later did he realize what was happening.

As they worked, they talked about who had been there and who had not, and about which church members had not attended for several weeks. They shared names of newcomers to the worship service, or perhaps one individual who showed up in a class somewhere. They shared the chance comments—good and bad—they had heard. They reviewed it all.

In that seemingly wasteful exercise, which George felt was far beneath his calling, the staff was, in fact, taking a "line-by-line, item-by-item analysis" and discovering assignments for the week: who needed to be followed up on, which visits were most critical, what phone calls or actions deserved top priority, what adjustments in the program were necessary.

In a large church, people can easily get lost in the cracks. But it can happen in a smaller church, too. Even a church with fewer than 50 in attendance.

One exercise I set for myself my first years in small churches was to personally mail out bulletins on Monday morning to those absent the previous day. I often wrote, "I missed you." Or "Hope your trip went well." Or "Here's something you might be interested in," circling the item.

It took several hours of time, but it kept me right on top of the "inventory" of the rich treasure entrusted to my care as pastor.

Numbers matter. Even one matters. Jesus said that.

Numbers matter for another reason. Numbers can tell us things. We depend on them in almost every field: business, industry, science.

We say we are interested in quality, not in quantity. Yet in almost every field *we measure quality by quantity*.

As far as I know, there is no evidence in medical history that a thermometer ever healed anyone.

But in medicine, doctors and nurses take vital signs: temperature, pulse, respiration, blood pressure. EKGs, blood and urine tests, X rays, electroencephalograms, and other diagnostic testing is done. And on the basis of such tests, a doctor proceeds.

My kids, who are baseball fans, can tell you the batting average—figured out to thousandths—on any given Sunday afternoon for almost every single major league player. They know earned-run averages and the standings. In sports, we measure quality by quantity, and we have reams of material on it daily that many men, at least, commit to memory and discuss with joy and great excitement.

A harsh example of measuring is the *bathroom scale*. I can give up Frosties at Wendy's and quit eating between snacks. But I step on those scales, and they tell me things I do not want to know.

My father was pastor of a church in Wenatchee, Washington, when I was in junior high school. When my father left in 1948, the church had a membership of 649, a worship attendance of 257, and a church school attendance of 235. In 1968 I was back at that church for a week's preaching mission. In 1978 I was there again for a special dedication program.

It is a strong church. Good families. Lay people who have served on denominational committees. They have had strong pastoral leadership and a fine church plant. To look out over that congregation on a Sunday morning is inspiring.

But look at the figures on this graph. Lay a paper at

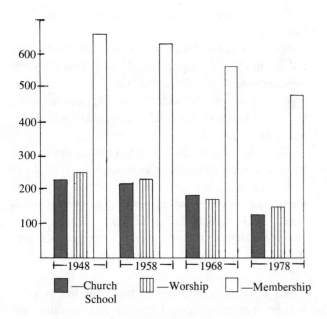

Wenatchee Valley Brethren
Baptist Church United

the tops of the "worship" and "church school" columns, so that the edge of the paper just touches the top right corners of the "worship" columns. The graph covers three decades. Look where that paper takes you in the next three decades if the trend continues. That church will not survive . . . unless it experiences a dramatic turnaround.

The graph tells us other things. Back when my father was pastor, there was a large gap between membership and attendance. Church Growth people project that about 200 to 350 people are all that one person can adequately pastor.[5] In 1948 there was trouble on the horizon because two-thirds of the membership was inactive, not drawn into the life of the church in a vital way.

We have also drawn graphs for the two churches I now serve. We did one for the Panorama City church

from 1945, the year it began. As you look at it, you see a portrait of a church. A chart is as valuable as any doctor's set of X rays.

You see the early growth which often comes to a new congregation. You see periodic dips when a new pastor came and the heading back up only after people and pastor began to work together. You see the church school foretelling what happened in worship, as the experts predict.

Any church serious about its future will engage in such studies.

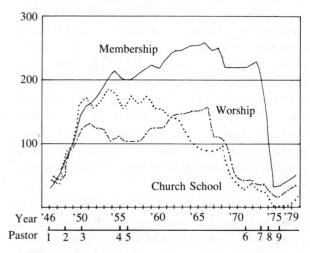

Panorama City Church of the Brethren

Numbers matter very much in the health of our physical bodies and in the health of the Body of Christ, the church.

Assumption 4: Workable strategies exist. They are Biblical and they can be monitored.

How could the apostle Paul accomplish so much in ten short years? Did he simply head out, empowered with the Holy Spirit, with no plan, no idea where he would head or what he was about?

Roland Allen, in a book first published in 1912 entitled *Missionary Methods: St. Paul's or Ours?*[6], suggested that growth in the New Testament church was not accidental. Paul, he argued, had a very careful strategy for growth. We may argue about some of Allen's conclusions, but he is convincing when he proceeds to list these observations from Acts:

16

Paul limited his work to Rome-administered areas.

He focused on two or three centers in each area.

He went to centers of Jewish influence.

In new communities, he used contacts supplied by relatives of people from established churches.

He reached whole families.

In our next chapter we will explore together some of the key strategies that become important for our own task. And we will see how utterly Biblical they are.

Teaching Helps for Chapter 3

Before the class session:

☐ Secure figures for your congregation for the past 11 years for resident active membership, church school, and worship. Ask someone to bring a calculator.

☐ Prepare these overhead transparencies: "Assumptions," "People Need," "The Scriptures Say," "We Have Offered," "Christ Is Not Pleased" and "Growth in the New Testament."

☐ Prepare copies of Medical Charts 2 through 5 for each participant.

Suggested Lesson Plan

1. Using the "Assumptions" transparency, discuss each of the author's assumptions, presenting material from the text for each in your own words.

• "Our Christian faith is the most important thing we have to share." Use the "People need" overhead and give opportunity for discussion. Follow with "The Scriptures Say" and "We Have Offered."

• "Evangelism is more than seeking."

Discuss: "Have you spent a recent day shopping but not buying? How did you feel about the use of that day? How would you feel about loading a grocery cart, but not pushing it through the checkout counter?"

Read together the "Christ Is Not Pleased" overhead. Assign each Scripture (given in the text) to a group of two or three people. Ask them to select a word or phrase that summarizes Christ's displeasure with the event. Have each respond if they feel this really does apply to what Christ wants of us. Do these Scriptures apply to church growth?

• "Numbers matter."

Name practical reasons why numbers matter in your church group (how much food to prepare for supper; how many books to buy for church school; how many chairs to set for a meeting; etc.).

Discuss: "How do you react to the statement 'Every number has a name'? What about 'God loves each of us as if there were only one of us'?

"In what way does our church take a line-by-line, item-by-item analysis for follow-up assignments?"

• "There are workable strategies."

Do you already have any spoken or unspoken strategies?

List figures for your church membership, worship attendance, and church school attendance in 1948, 1958, 1968, and 1978. Then discuss: "Why does a church need to grow constantly even to remain at the same level? How does this correspond to cell growth in the human body?"

List three reasons why the church school is a predictor of growth.

Have students look up Scriptures to discover how the early church insured growth. See Acts 2:46, 47; Acts 4:23-31, 33; Acts 5:42; Acts 6:4, 7; Acts 8:4, 30; Acts 9:17, 20; Acts 10:48; Acts 11:19-21. Assign each of the Scriptures to one or several students. (Discoveries may be: teaching new believers, staying with them until they have full understanding, praying, receiving the presence of Christ—the Holy Spirit—as a guide for daily life.)

Share findings in the group. How can you use this understanding?

Discuss the "Growth in the New Testament" overhead.

2. Come prepared with the figures for the past 11 years in your congregation. Have someone read the figures, and have each person write them on Medical Chart 2.

—First, the dates across the top.

—Second, the membership at the end of each

year. Use resident communicant membership.

—Third, the morning worship attendance average. Do not estimate. (Someone has said, "The best way to increase attendance is to estimate.")

—Fourth, the church school attendance average.

—Finally, the "composite membership"—the three figures for each year added together and divided by three.

3. Fill out Medical Chart 3 together.

First, have them transfer the *membership* figures from Chart 2 and write them in squares at the top of Chart 3. They will need to place the dates across the bottom. You might suggest the increments to use up the left-hand side; note the highest number to be recorded, and make sure that whatever increments you use will allow for it as you plot the membership line over the 11 years. Plot the number for each year at the appropriate spot on the graph with a dot or an X, then connect the marks from left to right across the page.

Second, do the same for *worship.*

Third, do the same for *church school.*

4. Fill out the *composite membership* graph on Medical Chart 4, using the numbers from the bottom box on Medical Chart 2.

5. Have someone figure out the percent of increase or decrease for each year, using a calculator. (To do this, subtract the earlier year's composite membership from the latter year's membership. Divide by the earlier year. Then multiply this answer by 100; this changes the decimal to percent.)

Example: 100 members in 1980
          110 members in 1981

Step 1. 110 − 100 = 10

Step 2. 10 ÷ 100 = .10

Step 3. .10 × 100 = 10% annual growth rate

Record each year's percent on Medical Chart 5. Again, mark the number for each year with a dot at the appropriate spot on the graph, and connect the dots from left to right with a line. Talk about what you have recorded. What does it say? If it is a straight line, remember that a normal, healthy church in North America should grow at a rate of 5 percent per year.*

6. Read together Luke 15:1-7. What does this story of Jesus say about the importance of numbers? Talk about it. (Thoughts expressed by participants on Luke 15 might include the importance of one; the fact that the shepherd would not even have known one was missing had he not taken a regular "line-by-line" analysis of his sheep. Notice his refusal to be satisfied with 99 if even one was lost. But let each person share what he finds there.)

---

*Medical Charts 2, 3, 4, 5, and 11 are adapted with permission from materials produced by Carl George of the Charles E. Fuller Institute of Evangelism and Church Growth. For a more extensive look at these areas, see also Bob Waymire and Peter Wagner, *The Church Growth Survey Handbook,* published by the Global Church Growth Bulletin, P.O. Box 66, Santa Clara, CA 95052.

1. Donald A. McGavran, *Understanding Church Growth, Fully Revised* (Grand Rapids: Eerdmans, 1980), p. 24.
2. In an interview with Michael Jackson on radio KABC, September 26, 1980.
3. See McGavran, *Understanding* . . . p. 15.
4. Miles K. Ketchum, "Rescue Management—A New Solution to an Old Problem," *The Journal of Commercial Banking and Lending,* December 1980, p. 27.
5. See discussion in chapter 5.
6. Roland Allen, *Missionary Methods: Saint Paul's or Ours?* republished (Grand Rapids: Eerdmans, 1962).

Assumptions

Our Christian faith is the most important thing we have to share.

Evangelism is more than "seeking."

Numbers matter.

There are workable strategies:

- **They are BIBLICAL.**
- **They can be monitored.**

People need
- bread
- justice
- peace

but even more, they need

- ground on which to stand
- a faith around which to orient their lives

THE SCRIPTURES

say that people can survive all kinds of physical hardship if they have faith!

HUNGER • PRISON
OPPRESSIVE GOVERNMENTS • SICKNESS
LOSS OF GOODS • DEATH ITSELF

But physical well-being without faith is utterly disastrous.

WE HAVE OFFERED

Peace
without the peacemaker;

Service
without the servant;

Knowledge
without the mind of Christ;

Equality, Liberation, Respectability
without the cross as a leveling experience;

Fellowship and Ecumenicity
without knowing Christ as Brother and God as Father.

CHRIST IS NOT PLEASED WITH...

- Fishing without catching.
- Empty banquet tables.
- Sowing without reaping.
- A fig tree that bears no fruit.
- Lost sheep that are not brought into the fold.
- A lost coin that is sought but not found.
- Harvests that are not reaped.
- Proclamation without response.
- Sons and daughters outside the Father's house.

Growth in the New Testament church was not by accident.

PAUL HAD
A PLAN,
A STRATEGY
FOR GROWTH:

- He limited himself to Rome-administered areas.
- He focused in two or three centers in each area.
- He went to centers of Jewish influence.
- In new communities, he used contacts supplied by relatives of people from established churches.
- He reached whole families.

Medical Chart 2
A Thorough Physical for Your Congregation

FILL IN DATES FOR PAST 11 years										
19__	19__	19__	19__	19__	19__	19__	19__	19__	19__	19__

RESIDENT MEMBERSHIP AS OF END OF EACH YEAR ABOVE										

MORNING WORSHIP ATTENDANCE AVERAGE— 52 SUNDAYS										

CHURCH SCHOOL ATTENDANCE AVERAGE— 52 WEEKS										

COMPOSITE MEMBERSHIP— YEARLY AVERAGE OF THE ABOVE DATE (add the 3 figures for each year and divide by 3)										

Medical Chart 3
Membership, Worship, and Church School Change

MEMBERSHIP

19__	19__	19__	19__	19__	19__	19__	19__	19__	19__	19__

WORSHIP

19__	19__	19__	19__	19__	19__	19__	19__	19__	19__	19__

CHURCH SCHOOL

19__	19__	19__	19__	19__	19__	19__	19__	19__	19__	19__

___											
___											
___											
___											
___											
___											
___											
___											
___											
___											
___											
___											
___											
___											

19__	19__	19__	19__	19__	19__	19__	19__	19__	19__	19__

Medical Chart 4
Composite Membership Change

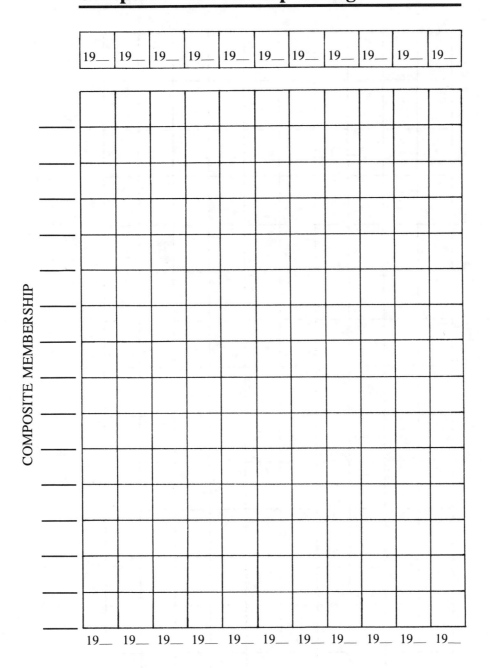

19__	19__	19__	19__	19__	19__	19__	19__	19__	19__	19__

COMPOSITE MEMBERSHIP

19__ 19__ 19__ 19__ 19__ 19__ 19__ 19__ 19__ 19__ 19__

Medical Chart 5
Annual Composite Percent of Change

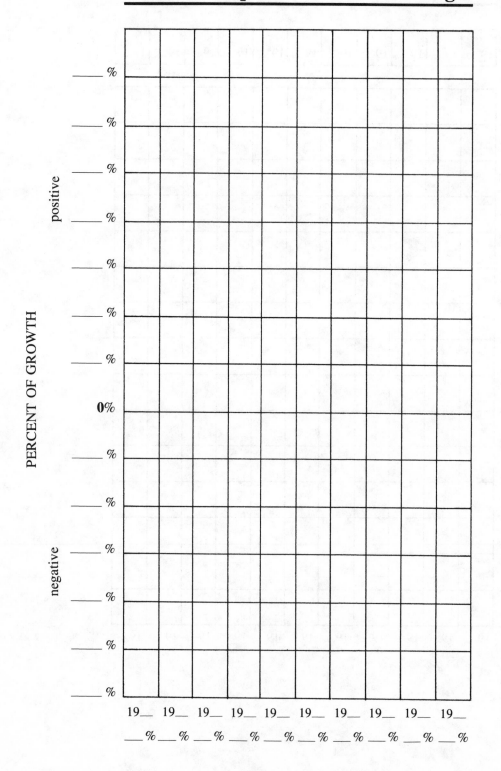

4 Some Strategies

When Eddie Gibbs of the British Bible Society conducts growth seminars among Anglicans in England, he begins by saying, "I am not here to entertain you nor even to inform you. I am here that your church might grow. If it does not grow as a result of our time together, this will have been a waste of your time and of mine."

The things we are about to suggest will seem very simple. But they do work. They are backed up by a lot of research in many countries, among many peoples around the world. There are technical terms that have been developed for some of them. We will share them as simply as possible.

Strategy 1: Go to the groups you are best suited to reach.

This is basic New Testament strategy. Read it for yourself. Andrew brought his brother, Peter (Jn. 1: 40, 41). The Samaritan woman brought her village (Jn. 4: 28-30). Jesus called Matthew, a tax collector. Soon after that, many other tax collectors were dining with Jesus and following Him (Mk. 2: 14, 15). A sinful woman was forgiven. Soon other sinful women found their way to Jesus (Lk. 7: 37-8: 3). People brought their families, their friends, those among whom they worked.

In the modern church, we often make evangelism so difficult—as if we must go to total strangers, knock on strange doors.

I conducted a growth seminar in a little church in southern Iowa. Many of those attending were from very small towns. The host church was in a town with a population of 76. I thought to myself, *Am I laying heavy guilt on people whose churches cannot possibly grow?* Then I thought some more and realized that some of them were public school-teachers. They had numerous contacts. Others sold their grain and bought products from associates not far away. A few were professional people. But all of them had unchurched friends with whom they worked every day.

It all starts with one person who wins a friend. The friend tells one or two more. And they bring a relative or neighbor and so on, like the old shampoo ad on television where faces fill the screen.

The place to start is not far away. *Go to the people you know the best.*

I have a friend who sells encyclopedias. After each sale he asks if the person has any friends who might also be interested. Most of his sales come from such leads.

The Mormons are discovering this. For well over 100 years they have sent their finest young men to go from door to door. But now their studies reveal that where they go "cold," with no previous contact or social network, the conversion success rate is 0.1 percent, or one in every 1,000 visits.

If, however, that missionary visit occurs within the home of a Mormon's relative or friend, the odds of success increase to 50 percent, one in every two visits.[1]

We do best with those we know. Start there.

Strategy 2: Go to the receptive people.

One of the discoveries of Church Growth experts is that all people are not receptive all the time. We are more receptive at some periods of our lives than others. And receptivity does not last forever.[2]

Jesus knew about this. When He instructed His disciples to move on down the road if a village did not receive them, He was saying, "Go where people will listen." The ones who are open to what you have to say—"he that hath ears to hear"(Mt. 11: 15)—are the ones where you need to focus your efforts.

The apostle Paul knew this. He talked of doors being closed. Rather than standing around banging on them, he moved on to find open doors (see, for example, Acts 16: 6-10).

How helpful this has been in my ministry. During the early years in the small churches I serve, I went after the membership rolls, people who had been members but were not there now. Evening after evening and Saturday after Saturday, I would get to know the people, try to win their friendship, try to lure them back. They were not interested. They had reinvested their lives in other things. Later, maybe, but not now.

The Church Growth advice is to hold unreceptive peoples lightly. To badger is to drive them away. Love them. Let them know you care. But like unripe fruit or harvests not yet "white" (Jn 4:35), keep a caring eye on them, and wait.

If you would grow, *spend your time with receptive people.*

The experts have become very detailed and technical in this area, developing a "resistance-receptivity axis" and talking of "right end" (or "receptive") people. Each year a book is published listing the unreached people and identifying which are resistant and which are receptive.[3] A student of growth in Indonesia said, "I can tell you where to go in Indonesia and labor for years with virtually no results. And I can tell you where people are responsive and ready."

I DID IT MY WAY.

But we don't need to be all that detailed to know where to begin. Here are some obvious clues.

Visitors to your church are more receptive than those with no contact with the church. That should be obvious. But most churches do not act on it. If you can return their visit *within 48 hours* when their interest level is highest, the odds are far greater that they will come back than if you wait a week or more. Your visit to them should be low-key, friendly,

learning to know them, where they work, how long they have lived in the area, their interests. Simply let them know you are glad they came.

Most of us are not structured for this. We know who teaches church school. We know who takes up the offering and who counts the offering. But who in your church is responsible for the guest book, for getting the name and address of every new person who visits? And who is responsible for visiting them within that all-important 48 hours?

Changes are often times of receptivity: a new home, a new child, a new job, living in a new community, the death of some loved one, a serious illness, or when the first child enters school. Caring people will be sensitive to these and available.

When people move into your community, they have left friends, organizations, and structures of their lives. They are often lonely, looking for new places to put down their roots, more open to new possibilities than they have been for a long time.

Win Arn talks of "Mary's wonder bread." Mary was not granted the spiritual gift of being an evangelist. But she was gifted as a baker of wonderful homemade bread. Every time a new family moved into her neighborhood, she was there to greet them with a fresh-baked loaf of bread. And as a result of her simple, friendly visit and that rich-smelling, hot, homemade bread, quite a few of her new neighbors found their way into the church.

Children often are more receptive between the ages of 10 and 12 than are youth between the ages of 15 and 17. Many cultures have ceremonies to symbolize the transitions to adulthood. At 11, 12, or 13, African tribal rites, Jewish bar mitzvahs, and, in some churches, Christian baptism or confirmation recognize that those years are crucial to the directions of later life. Roy Burkhart in the huge First Community Church in Columbus, Ohio, had a special yearlong focus—"The Fellowship of the Block of Wood"—for children as they entered junior high. You may feel your church is not large enough to have this kind of focus. But many a rabbi spends countless hours one-on-one with students studying to become a "son of the Law." You can, too.

People with felt needs you can meet will be more receptive than people with other needs. John Wimber, while pastor of Yorba Linda Friends Church in California, said that if he were to start a new congregation, he would do it within a mile of Bob Schuller's Crystal Cathedral, and he would attempt to meet needs that giant church is not meeting. His church took a survey of young parents who lived in its area. What do you think was the number one felt need of those parents? Marriage counseling? Child raising? What?

The number one need uncovered in their survey was potty training for their children. So the church found a well-qualified teacher and offered a course in toilet training. They used Proverbs 22:6 on their brochure: "Train up a child in the way he should go. . . ." Really!

Robert Schuller says the key to his success is "Find a need and fill it. Find a hurt and heal it." People with felt needs that you can meet are often receptive people.

Friends of converts are often receptive.

The Mormons have carefully studied the success ratio when their young missionaries visit strangers in the homes of the missionaries' friends. As a result of these studies, they have begun to instruct their laity to engage first in building close personal ties to neighbors and associates. Often they admonish them to avoid or downplay a discussion of religion. Warm, personal bonds come first. Theology must come later.

Be alert to times of receptivity and invest your time primarily on those who are receptive. But know that receptivity does not last forever. It passes. A day, a week, a month may be too long. *Strike while the iron is hot,* if you would reach people.

Strategy 3: Use the tools you have.

People feel separated from the church by fear, uncertainty, misconceptions, bad memories, guilt. They remember the church the way it was ten years ago, the last time they were present. They feel ashamed even to think of entering. How will they be received? Will they suddenly be surrounded as if by a swarm of killer bees?

I have discovered some *natural bridges* to bring people into the church.

Usually when someone says "evangelism" immediately we think, "Oh, she means Billy Graham," or, "Aha, he wants me to go knock on doors."

Donald McGavran in the 1930's drew heavily on the research of a Methodist bishop, J. W. Pickett, who discovered that *how* people made their entrance into the church mattered far less ten years down the road than the kind of postbaptismal care they received along the way.[4] Some came for *social* reasons—because a friend or relative was coming. Some came for *selfish* reasons—because they felt it gave them social standing or prestige or economic advantage. They came for a wide variety of reasons, only a few of which were *genuinely religious*. But later these reasons became almost indistinguishable. What mattered far more was whether they had been loved and carefully taught and challenged and nurtured once they were there.

A few years ago we began a denominational night at Dodger Stadium. Not only do our members go, but we encourage people to bring neighbors and friends. We assume that it is OK for Christians to have fun together, that an evening of fellowship among scattered churches in Southern California is a worthy endeavor.

One grandmother brought 14 children and grandchildren who had not been a part of the church in recent years.

We invited our neighbors across the street, a couple with children ages 9 and 11. They had not been in any church for almost nine years, since their youngest was a baby. One Sunday as they sat on a front pew in a church, someone from the nursery had brought their screaming infant all the way up front to deposit the child with them. They said, "This is not for us," and never went back.

But they went with our church group to that Dodger night. They also took along half a dozen friends from work.

Six months later, my neighbor said to me, "We're going to start coming to your church." I thought,

"Sure you are." But several Sundays later, they were there. After church they called us over to ask all kinds of questions. Except for a few weeks when they have been away, they have attended virtually every major function of our church since their first visit.

Our little church has had a *family night* once a month, a covered-dish meal followed by some simple, light program. Our neighbors brought her mother, some of her mother's friends, and several friends of their own to that informal evening. The mother joined the church, sings in the choir, and leads a crafts group.

Each summer my neighbor coaches a Little League baseball team. He told the father of one of his players that our church was forming a men's softball team.

"But we don't go to church," the man said. "We can take care of that," my neighbor replied.

One Sunday a woman walked into church. Early that week I visited her in her home. She said to me, "That's the first time any pastor has ever visited me after attending a church."

I asked her how she happened to come to our church. As a girl, she said, she had gone to church. Her husband, who had recently died, had never gone to church and had wanted her to stay home Sundays with him. After he died, some friends invited her to a mother-daughter banquet in their tiny little church in Missouri. They treated her so well, showed her such love, that she vowed to join a church of the same denomination when she moved to California, if she could find one. She is now a member, attends every Sunday, and is a member of our church board.

These are natural bridges into the church. They are as simple as the invitation of the disciples when they told friends about Jesus: "Come and see" (Jn. 1:46). No need to argue theology or try to prove something. Come, see and experience a group of people who have something I find of value.

Studies reveal that each of us has an average personal prospect list of 8.4 people: friends, neighbors, associates at work or school, and relatives.[5] We all know people who do not go to church, who are not active, responsible disciples. We all know people who, with some friendship and a right approach, would become living members of Christ's Church.

Approach them as though you were a masterful fisherman. Cultivate friendship first. Build strong personal ties. Then think what would be a natural, easy way for them to be introduced to the fellowship. Choose the bait, the best lure, like a fisherman. And allow time. With my neighbor, it took six months.

If each Christian won just one person this year, the Church would double in size.

Yet the sad truth is that *95% of all Christians* in North America *will not win one person to Christ during their entire lifetimes!*[6]

Use the tools you have.

Families may be a bridge. McGavran points out that the best growth overseas is through families. When a wife can come with her husband and children as an entire family, their decision is far stronger, with far less pain and social disruption, much more apt to be stable and lasting, than if only one person comes through what McGavran calls "drip by drip" evangelism.[7]

In the New Testament, entire households often entered the church at one time.[8] My father, serving a church in industrial Lima, Ohio, during World War II, observed that if a child came alone, that child rarely stayed on unless the family was also won.

Use the tools you have.

New people are the best evangelists, for several reasons. Their *excitement* is high. They have a deep *commitment level*. They have many *outside contacts*. And perhaps most important of all, they *know the way in*. They can help explain things to those who are new to the faith.

If you would grow, draw on the resources of your newest people. More than any others, they have many contacts back into the non-Christian world.

Strategy 4: Don't dump the whole load at once.

Meet people where they are and *love them*. Take them where they are and *trust God to lead them*. Take them where they are and *give them the freedom to struggle and grow*, just as you have demanded that kind of freedom for yourself.

They are babes. They don't know all that it means to be a Christian. They will drink milk for a while. Later they will begin to take solid food.

They have much to learn. They need much patience. They need a strong arm of love around them. They need time.

I am 49 years old. I was baptized at age 9. Across 40 years I have been challenged in many areas, and I have grown as a Christian. If I expect my neighbor, new to the faith, to swallow all I have come to learn and struggle with and know across 40 years, I am grossly unfair.

How do you eat an elephant? One bite at a time.

We shut people out when we demand too much too soon. *Begin at the point of their felt need.* Go with them step by step, giving God a chance to work His own special miracles in their lives.

Strategy 5: Keep evangelism high.

Churches tend to grow to a certain level of attendance and then plateau.

Lyle Schaller has diagramed some plateaus, based on rather careful research. Most churches in our country tend to cluster around worship attendance at 30 to 35. The next cluster comes at 70 to 85. The next at 115 to 135. Then 175 to 200. And so on.[9]

The question is, how do you move a congregation up to the next level of worship attendance? Only through major effort. The only way our Panorama City church, which now is at 30 to 35, can move up to the next level is by doing things *now* in certain key areas that a church of 70 to 85 would do. Yet we must do them with only 30 to 35 people.

What do I mean?

For one thing, we have no nursery. Only one of our families has a baby, and they usually hold him in church when they come. Yet we know that if we are to grow, we must equip and staff a nursery now.

We have only one church school class for grades one through six. The age span is far too great. If we are to grow, we must begin to staff at least two classes in that span, even though at first we may have no children in one of those classes on some Sundays.

But how can we, with our present membership, begin to act now like a church at that next level? The only way this can happen is by *going on a diet.* We must *starve ourselves* of many "good" things in order that we may achieve the growth we want.

I sat in a meeting a year ago in Glendale as person after person suggested things we ought to be doing. Programs should be expanded, fellowship activities multiplied. But none of these was related to the tasks I knew we had to do if we were to grow.

I tried as best I could to spell it out, to challenge them to literally *starve* themselves for a time of some good things in order to have what they had all agreed was the *best* thing, the number one priority item on their list at the time.

In all of life, good things crowd out the best. One of the definitions of sin in the Bible is choosing the lower in the face of the higher.

If you would grow, keep your focus. Debt retirement can consume all your energy. One man came in and insisted we start weekly square dancing. Another person had a dream for something else.

Know your goals. Keep them clear. Know what must be done to move in the direction of those goals, or you will flounder.

I like Marilyn Koehler's statement of Jesus' style of ministry:

> He never organized mass meetings;
>   never went door to door;
>   never buttonholed a person;
>   never judged people weighed down with sin.
> He ministered to the whole person;
>   met people where they were;
>   tried to give a vision of what they could be.
> He said, "As you go . . ."
>   He went naturally.
>   His disciples reached out to those they knew.

Teaching Helps for Chapter 4

Before the session:

☐ Discuss with the chairman of your church board or pastor how best to feed ideas from this study group to the church.

☐ Prepare these overhead transparencies: "Strategies," "Receptive Times," "Natural Bridges (A and B)" and "Plateaus."

☐ Prepare copies of Medical Charts 6 and 7 for each participant.

☐ In preparation for *next* week, ask someone who has never attended your congregation to come for worship unannounced and unknown. Then have the "mystery guest" report to your class next week, telling how he was received, his impressions, and what things would make him want to come again or content never to return.

Suggested Lesson Plan

1. Look together at the transparency on "Strategies." Discuss what each strategy would mean for you.

   ● "Go to the groups you are best suited to reach."

Discuss: "What are the groups in our community that we are best suited to reach?"

Have someone relate the story of Cornelius in Acts 10 and reflect on what persons or group you could reach if empowered by God's Spirit. What is the least likely group to enter your doors?

"Name three daily contacts whose life-style is dissimilar to yours. Would they be challenged by the Good News?"

   ● "Go to the receptive peoples."

Show the "Receptive Times" overhead. Then:

List some of the receptive people around you who ought to be on your priority list. Allow three minutes for this list making.

List some of the ways you might respond to their receptivity.

What about visitors to your congregation? Who is responsible for your guest book (and follow-up)? If no one is doing this, name someone to get every visitor's name and address each week.

Does your church community include people coping with new babies, children entering kindergarten, recent deaths, hospitalizations, terminal illnesses, new neighbors? Who is responsive to these needs?

What is the most pressing need of people within a five-block or two-mile radius of your church? How could you find out?

Hand out Medical Chart 6. Ask everyone to put his name in the center circle and then follow directions 1 through 4. Allow enough time for each step so that it will be completed thoughtfully.

Then talk together about whom you have chosen. Compare strategies. Are you willing to covenant with each other to each win one?

   ● "Use the tools you have."

Show "Natural Bridges—A" alone while you discuss: "What are our natural bridges?" Together suggest some and have each participant write them in on Medical Chart 7. Then add the transparency overlay ("Natural Bridges—B") to include the author's suggestions.

   ● "Don't dump the whole load at once."

Discuss: "Are we willing to take people where they are, love them, trust God to lead them, and do our part by providing the best possible Christian nurture? What should we *not* do"

   ● "Keep evangelism high."

Look at the "Plateaus" overhead. At what point are you?

Ask each person to make a list, on a separate piece of paper, of five things your congregation must do to move on to the next highest plateau. Allow three minutes for this.

To do these things and move to the next plateau, you will probably need to go on a "diet." Ask each person to list five things you will have to put aside for now.

Share what you have written with each other. Can you agree on three items in each category? Plan to present these to your board or governing body.

Review the strengths from Medical Chart 1 in this light. Should some of them be added now as natural bridges (Medical Chart 7) or areas on which to build?

2. Consider the "Jesus style of ministry" overhead. How do you feel about this statement?

Read together the Great Commission (Mt. 28:19, 20). Consider the imperative in the Greek: Literally Jesus said, "As you go, make disciples, baptizing, teaching. . . ." What do these parting words of the risen Lord mean for us?

Reflect on this observation: "When the resurrected Christ gave the commission to 'go, make disciples,' it was to be the primary work of every congregation, every member, everywhere."

1. "From the Editor," *Church Growth: America* (November-December, 1980), page 2.
2. Donald A. McGavran, *Understanding Church Growth: Fully Revised* (Grand Rapids: Eerdmans, 1980), pp. 245 ff.
3. C. Peter Wagner and Edward R. Dayton, editors, *Unreached Peoples '79* (Elgin: David C. Cook, 1978)
4. McGavran, *Understanding* . . . p. 364.
5. From research by Robert Orr, in Charles Arn, Donald McGavran, Win Arn, *Growth: A New Vision for the Sunday School* (Pasadena: Church Growth Press, 1980), p. 76.
6. Floyd G. Bartel, *A New Look at Church Growth* (Scottdale, Pa.: Mennonite Publishing House, 1979), p. 59.
7. McGavran, *Understanding,* pp. 359-363.
8. I Corinthians 1:16; Luke 19:9; John 4:52; Acts 10; Acts 18:8.
9. Lyle Schaller, *Hey, That's Our Church* (Nashville: Abingdon, 1975), p. 40.
See also Lyle Schaller, *Survival Tactics in the Parish* (Nashville: Abingdon, 1977), p. 52.

STRATEGIES

STRATEGIES

1. Go to the groups you are best suited to reach.
2. Go to the receptive people.
3. Use the tools you have.
4. Don't dump the whole load at once.
5. Keep evangelism high on your list of priorities.

RECEPTIVE TIMES

Moving to a New Community
— New friends
— New groups
— New schedule

A New Baby
Death of a Loved One
A Change in Marital Status
A Change in Job Status
Sickness
Hospitalization
First Child Enters School

Medical Chart 6
Develop Your Own Web.

1. Put your name in the center circle.
2. In the surrounding circles, enter the names of nonchurch people you know best, your own "8.4" prospect list of friends, neighbors, work or school associates, and relatives.
3. Then pick the one best prospect and write that person's name here: _____ .
4. Begin to list elements of your strategy to bring that person to Christ this year:

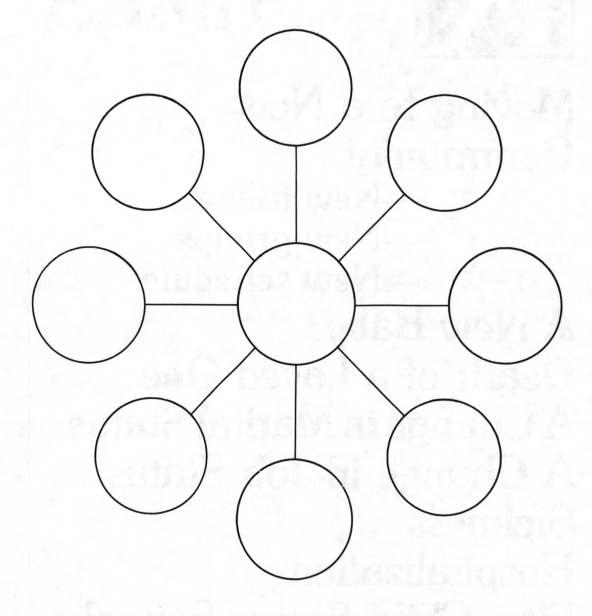

FEAR

UNCERTAINTY

MISCONCEPTIONS

BAD MEMORIES

GUILT

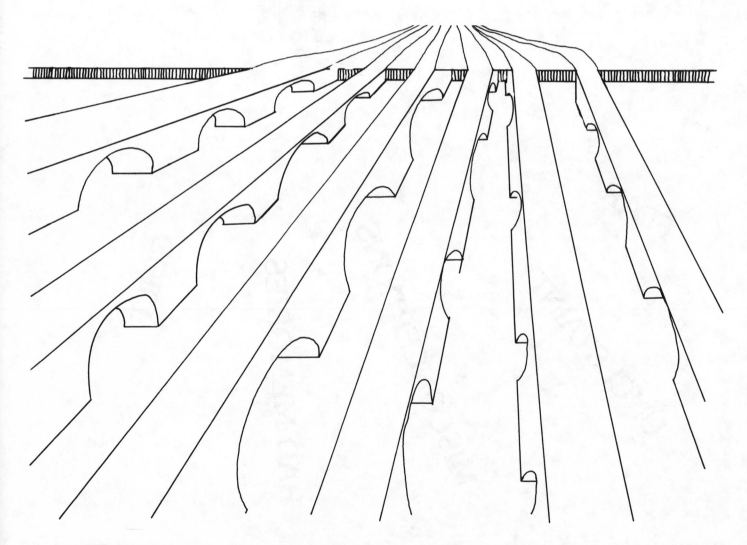

SOFTBALL TEAM

DODGER NIGHT

EASTER/CHRISTMAS CHORAL PROGRAMS

MOTHER/DAUGHTER NIGHT

FAMILY NIGHT

NOON MEALS

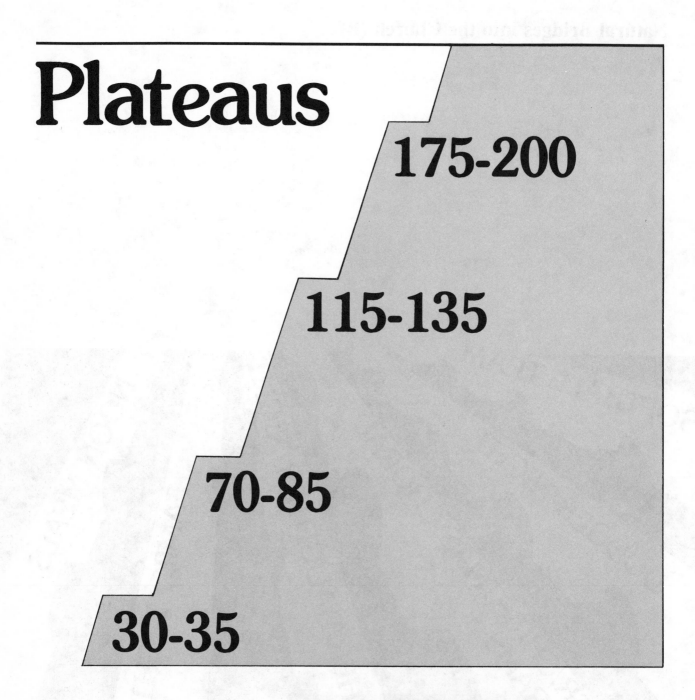

Plateaus

175-200

115-135

70-85

30-35

WORSHIP ATTENDANCE

THE *JESUS* STYLE OF MINISTRY

He never organized mass meetings;
never went door to door;
never buttonholed a person;
never judged people weighed down with
sin.
He ministered to the whole person;
met people where they were;
tried to give a vision of what they could
be.
He said, "As you go . . ."
He went naturally.
His disciples reached out to those they
knew: Andrew brought Peter,
Samaritan woman brought her
entire village.

5 Leadership, Followership, and Growth

Peter Wagner reduces the conditions needed for church growth listed in the introduction to three: Every church can grow (1) if the *pastor* wants the church to grow; (2) if the *people* want it to grow; (3) provided it is *not terminally ill*.

Many pastors do not want their churches to grow.

Why? Although they would never admit it even to themselves, deep down they know that the price of growth is too high.

It isn't that they set out *not* to grow. If a family moves away, they will scurry about to find a replacement. They help their congregation maintain its size, replenish itself. But aside from that, their activities trail off into other areas.

The Pastor's Price for Growth

Many have talked about the price of growth. In an excellent article in *Church Growth: America,* Peter Wagner detailed some of that cost for the pastor.[1]

First, it means *hard work. Long hours.* My observation is that the pastor, too, must go on a "diet." I know a pastor of a huge downtown church who for years acted in plays put on by a local semiprofessional theater group. Some pastors become chaplains to fire departments or even part-time fire fighters. Some run for school boards or give as much time to various community endeavors or service clubs as to their own congregations.

Growth requires a pastor's full attention.

Second, it means a willingness to *supplement inadequate training.* Most pastors are not trained in seminary in the principles of growth. The rough estimate is that it takes 300 to 400 hours of reading to become immersed enough to become an effective leader of the grass roots. This means time and money and special effort.

Third, there must be a willingness to put *leadership on the line.* We'll talk about this more later in the chapter.

Further, there must be a willingness to *share leadership,* to delegate, to involve others in key roles. I know a pastor who, in the last church he served, spent every evening and every weekend visiting, delegating almost all of the decision making to an excellent group of lay people. That church grew very rapidly, although it is a pattern quite different from many growing churches.

Fifth, the pastor must *be willing to have members whom others pastor.* Lyle Schaller uses the terms "shepherd" and "rancher."[2] As a church grows, others must be brought into the shepherding role—either paid staff or trained lay people. The pastor who insists on closely shepherding everyone personally cannot be pastor of a very large church.

Sixth, Wagner suggests, the pastor must be willing to *stick it out.* We'll discuss this one in greater detail in this chapter, too.

Profile of a Growth Pastor

Out of my experience, I have developed a profile of a Church Growth pastor.

1. *A hard worker.* Leads are followed. No stone is left unturned. When God opens a door, the pastor walks through. Tomorrow is too late.

2. *Always a student.* I set aside time every week for Church Growth reading. It enriches every area of my ministry and brings together some experiences that did not make sense before.

Church Growth is like photography. You can start with a simple camera with fixed settings and some darkroom trays and some jars of formula. And you can do excellent work. But you can go from that *as far as you want to go.* Church Growth is an exciting, gutsy, challenging, rewarding field.

There ought to be classes along the way, or some seminars from the Institute for American Church Growth as they provide them in your area.[3] There are some excellent magazines, such as *Church Growth: America.*[4] There is now a steady stream of excellent books. Start with McGavran's classic, *Understanding Church Growth,* or with one of the insightful and practical books by Peter Wagner, Lyle Schaller, Win Arn, or George Hunter.[5] But begin.

3. *Secure, not threatened.* There are twin dangers here. One is to be insecure and threatened by strong lay leadership. Coach Paul "Bear" Bryant of the

University of Alabama says he never hires anyone for his coaching staff who is *not* brighter than he. "If they're not brighter than I am, I don't need them." Pastors threatened by people who can teach a better lesson or think through some financial problem faster will forever shepherd small churches.

The other danger is to be so insecure as to be unwilling to move in on the hard problems, to fail to move to make the changes that *must be made* if the church is to progress.

4. *A person of vision.* Every growing church has a sense of direction. Many have a reason for being that can be stated in a single phrase. Many such pastors preach that theme repeatedly, changing only the title and illustrations. One referred to his vision for the church and said, "I preach that theme four times a year." "Where there is no vision, the people perish" (Prov. 29:18). Robert Schuller puts it in his own unique way, "To fail to plan is to plan to fail."[6]

5. *A person of faith.* When the storms come, there must be rock to stand on. And the storms do come.

6. *Disciplined,* using energies and time very wisely. I have to make a list every day of what I want to do, in the order of the most important down to what could wait, if necessary.

7. *Very stubborn.* Dogged determination.

The Congregation's Price

But the congregation has a price to pay also. Wagner[7] lists four areas:

First, a church must *provide the dollars.* It costs money to get the basic training. It takes dollars to provide films and study books for the congregation. It takes dollars to do the things that you will begin to see must be done if your church is to grow.

Our Glendale church, for example, has its "front" doors at the back. The front of the sanctuary is right next to the street, while the entrance opens onto the parking lot behind. People had come to our church, walked around it and left because they could not figure out how to get in. Simple things like *signs* cost dollars.

Second, a church must be willing to *follow a growth leader.* Following toward growth can be painful at times, causing a reordering of lives.

Third, it must be willing to *give time and energy.* Dean Kelley was quoted in our introduction as saying most of us prefer things the way they are. It is so much easier and more peaceful to be part of a plateaued church.

Fourth, it must be willing to *sacrifice some fellowship.*

I recall a Christian from a church in Pomona, California, who attended a growth seminar. Her church is a beautiful one with an excellent pastor. But it had lost many members across the years, and the lovely sanctuary was now only about one-fourth full on a Sunday morning. She confided to me that after the growth seminar she had a dream. "One night I dreamed I came to church the next Sunday and the church was full of people. Strangers. I did not recognize one of them. Every seat was taken. Those of us who are members met at the back and went into the small chapel to have our own service. There was no room for us there anymore."

Some tight-knit circles need to be opened if a church is to grow. And for some, that is a price too high to pay.

Profile of a Growth Congregation

The *profile of a Church Growth congregation,* then, looks like this:

1. *Loving.* People in growing churches care about people. They genuinely love others. Some churches are able to fake it, I have discovered. A dozen or so people genuinely care and are reaching out. These few make it look as though the entire congregation cares.

But growth does not come through gimmicks. People sense genuine warmth and respond accordingly. Even people with different theological bents are drawn to folks who care about them. As one woman expressed it, "I go to that other church for its theology. But I keep coming back here because I feel I belong."

2. *Open*–to new people, to new ideas.

3. *Committed*. Earlier we noted Dean Kelley's observation that churches that make demands are strong, and strong churches grow.[8] Congregations that try to be everything to everybody end up being very little to anybody. In our troubled times, people are drawn to a fellowship of people who have a deep sense of direction and purpose.

You find this not by copying the theology or demands of some other church that happens to be growing. You find this by looking to your own tradition, your own best insights. Be yourself in the deepest, truest sense.

Rabbi Zushya, as he contemplated death, commented, "When I approach the divine throne, I will not be asked, 'Why were you not Moses?' I will be asked only, 'Why were you not Zushya?' "[9]

We did studies of growing and declining congregations in our own denomination.[10] The growing congregations felt better (by ratios of more than three to one) about themselves, their pastors, and their denominational beliefs than those that were declining.

My encyclopedia salesman friend says that the most important ingredient in selling is the salesperson's own enthusiasm and belief in the product. All the other training is secondary. He defines selling as getting the other person "to think as you think, to feel as you feel, and to act." If you don't feel it, you cannot get someone else to feel it either.

A growing congregation is committed.

4. *Flexible*. The seven last words of dying congregations are never heard on the lips of a growing one: "We never did it that way before."

They see changes that need to be made and are ready to make them. There is a health in their governing bodies, a willingness to "own" new ideas once presented rather than forever referring to an idea as "Dave's idea." Once it is shared, it belongs to the group. There is a willingness to make decisions and stick by them. Decisions are not reopened again and again. There is a high degree of trust. The focus is on the goal rather than on personalities and differences.

5. *Willing to change*–without compromising basic tenets, making room for readjustments.

6. *"Big" in attitude*. Sometimes churches are small in number because they are small in spirit. A petty, picky mood pervades. They scarcely want to be there themselves. Or they love the fights.

Big people think big, act big. Their congregations do not stay little very long. Take away the membership of many vibrant churches but leave some of the key people, and within a short time these churches will be booming and vibrant again.

We build in our own image.

The Ingredient of Patience

Robert Hymers, superintendent of the rapidly growing congregations of the Open Door Community Church of Los Angeles, talks in a very perceptive paper about the concept of *"false starts."* [11] It is helpful to know that sometimes the church sputters, loses some members, and experiences some serious setbacks before solid upward growth begins. Sometimes it is necessary to build a new base. The long-term guardians of the fellowship may hold on too tightly. A new coalition sometimes needs to be built. Patience is needed until enough newer people are able to feed in the new blood and enthusiasm required.

John Wimber, in his new role as pastor again, has talked of keeping the "systems cool," of trying to minimize personal confrontations.

There is a need to put aside an *apocalyptic complex*. It is so easy for pastors and lay people to come to a meeting feeling that "This is it; this is the test. If it doesn't happen tonight, it's over." Sometimes you go home with high hopes, sometimes with a feeling of utter franticness and deep despair.

I discovered that I recovered from major surgery by inches—not all at once.

The French writer Colette said, "My most famous art is to wait. To gather up crumbs. To piece together fragments."[12]

We need to know when to wait and when to push again. No one can tell us that. We may know it instinctively. Most of us discover it the hard way, by

46

trial and by costly error.

A long time ago I heard a wonderful Christian educator, Virginia Fisher, talk about growth in the life of a child. She said, "Physical growth times are times of flying apart. When a child is growing most rapidly, that child is most impossible to live with."

That may apply at times to churches. Sometimes there is tension, fear, loss of some very precious securities, short tempers.

One man puzzled, "Why is it that just when we begin to grow, something happens to spoil it? Something erupts, tempers flare, people walk away, and we go back to square one."

Some patterns seem to develop in this regard.

The first is the *no-man's-land* that sometimes happens between the old-timers and the newcomers. (Lyle Schaller calls them "homesteaders" and "pioneers," but some of us have trouble remembering which is which.)[13]

New people may find they are welcomed. They feel the church is warm and caring, just what they have been looking for. But suddenly they discover that others feel that they have come in far enough. I have found this to be true in every congregation I have served, but it is more devastating in smaller churches.

As new people, they see things that those who have been around never saw. G. K. Chesterton once said he would like to enter his home like a second-story burglar, to see it new and fresh, as for the first time.

New people see the separation in the carpet at the front entrance and wonder why it isn't fixed. They see the peeling paint in the kitchen. They notice that the doors need painting, some windows need to be replaced.

Often they are willing to help. But they want to get at it. They don't want to wait for committees. They want to cut through miles of red tape.

They do not understand why a committee can make a decision, but then one person who has been around a long time goes ahead and does just the opposite and no one raises a voice to object. They discover that newcomers must abide by rules but old-timers don't need to.

Some new people are cut off before they ever get in. They find people turning their backs on them in conversations, telling them in a dozen subtle ways that they are not really included.

But for others, the difficulty comes after gaining entrance to the membership.

Newcomers may say things like, "It just doesn't feel the same anymore. The desire to be there and help is gone now." Or, "We have gone to every event since we have come, but we are not accepted." "They don't even remember our names." "Maybe this isn't the church for us." "Don't they want new people?" "They want our bodies and our money, but they aren't really interested in what we think." Or, "We don't want to be a part of a church run by a few families."

Many times you never have the luxury of hearing the reasons. People drop out and never say why. When you visit them, they give other excuses about being busy or sick or something else. Down deep they know they have not been included.

Churches that want to grow must learn that *new people will not fight their way in.* They must be accepted. Welcomed. Someone or several people must put an arm around them, stay with them, help them get ideas presented, interpret things to them, see that they are adopted as full members of the family.

Exclusion happens in large churches, too. In the largest church I served, the wife of one of the leading men said, "Who are all these new people in *our* church?" Sometimes the response of the old-timers is not belligerent at all but simply the feeling of "I'm not needed anymore." Other times it may erupt with anger: "No one will ever take that job from me!"

Sometimes the problem surfaces quietly, with great pain and soul searching. Sometimes it comes explosively. In some churches there is a veritable mine field—a no-man's-land—between the old-timers and the newcomers.

The solution must be persistence, a lot of stroking, and the courage to move ahead. Rescue or Turnaround Management talks of the great tact required.

The consultant who would help a business turn around must come as a friend, not as an adversary. That person "must be people-conscious, aware of easily bruised egos, and must emphasize the results that can be achieved through combined effort."[14]

Chaplain—Pastor—Leader

The second developing pattern relates to the role of the pastor. One discouraged newcomer who felt excluded and resigned from the board commented to me, "They haven't accepted you either."

In every church I have served it has taken three years before things began to happen. I visited people, learned to know them. I preached my little heart out and led in worship. I sat through all the meetings, "paying my dues."

But I needed to get to know the people—their needs, their potential. I needed to discover the areas where they could begin to take hold. And they needed to know me, come to trust me, see how I reacted under pressure, know that I would not start them down some strange, costly road and then abandon them.

Most pastorates proceed according to a pattern. They go from the minister as *chaplain to pastor to leader*.

Many congregations hire a *chaplain*—someone to care for the morning worship, say prayers at their gatherings, give God's blessing to what they do, represent them at community gatherings.

Then begins the role as *pastor*. Bit by bit, I was with people at the birth of a new baby, I stood by their hospital beds in times of sickness, I went to their homes in times of tension and personal need, I buried a member of their family and shared in their grief, I officiated at the weddings of their sons or daughters, baptized their children. Over a period of years I genuinely came to be their pastor.

Only then did they let me begin to be a *leader*. For some old-timers, this would never be. The leadership role is granted first by those who come to the church during the pastor's term of service. This is why a founding pastor has it so much easier. All who come have come in under that pastor's conditions.

As I visit new prospects, I talk about the church, my dreams, its potential. If they come in, they tend to buy into what I want to see happen. But those who have been around other pastors, having bought into other dreams, may not share my vision at all. Sometimes they change. Some *must* change if the pastor is to be able to effectively lead. Some never do.

In the first church I served, in inner-city Harrisburg, Penn., the neighborhood had changed from middle-class to lower-class white with a sprinkling of minorities. A long-term pastor had been a good-hearted revivalist with a theology that belonged to an earlier era. He was followed by another long-term pastor with a more easygoing manner. During his leadership, many of the people moved to the suburbs and were eager to have the church follow. After I had been there awhile, a consensus began to develop: We needed to provide a strong Sunday morning program for those who lived in the suburbs and to create a seven-day-a-week program for those who lived in the shadows of the church.

But as the new program took shape in our minds, it became evident that we needed a greatly expanded building, which required buying adjacent row houses and tearing them down. It would take considerable money. More than that, it would take a core of people ready to act.

Many who had come in under the man two pastorates before me wanted to do nothing. The church was adequate for their needs. Their children were grown. They were content that we had tiny church school rooms in a dark, damp basement. Ten toddlers were cramped in a room eight feet by ten feet.

Those who had come in during the pastorate immediately before me wanted to spend no money *there*. They said it would be like "pouring money down a rathole."

What was happening during those early years, I realized, was that I was building a new congregation in the midst of the old. Gradually new leadership was emerging: a young doctor just getting established, several junior executives in various businesses, and some older people who liked what they saw developing. I discovered that you do not go into an established congregation, unfold your plans, and move the church into high gear with a flourish.

Experts on growth all agree that a willingness to invest a longer period of years is critical to building a growing, vibrant church. Doctors, lawyers, hairstylists, gas station and restaurant and small business owners know that a practice—enough customers to survive—does not happen by moving every three to seven years. Many pastors are beginning to learn this, too.

Peter Wagner, in his excellent book *Your Church Can Grow,* says that in America, *the primary catalytic factor for growth in a local church is the pastor.* The second factor is a well-mobilized, responsive laity.[15]

The most effective years for leadership in most pastorates, experts agree, are years 5 through 14.[16] As a pastor earns leadership rights, there must be a willingness to *use* that leadership, to *risk* that leadership, to *put it on the line* at times, to *use the power* that has been earned and given. Some want to be loved so much that they fail to act when strong, decisive leadership is demanded.

Pastors of strong, growing churches are not forever looking out the corner of the eye for greener pastures. However small, however great the problems, they would rather be where they are than anyplace else in the world. And they will not mistake a lateral move (to another congregation with the same set of circumstances) nor even a call to a larger congregation as a call from God. God blesses the faithful worker. And that often means perseverance.

What happens after year 14 depends on several things. Ralph Sockman went to a church in New York City as a bright, young man straight from seminary and served there with distinction his entire life. He says, "I didn't change churches as many do. The congregation changed for me." The high mobility in that city meant that across his lifetime he preached to an ever-changing group of people.

Others serve with increasing effectiveness beyond year 14 because they continue to grow—to study, to

dream, to be alert, to entertain new and exciting ideas. They refuse to repeat themselves. In historian Arnold Toynbee's terms, they bring a new and fresh response to each new challenge. Roy Burkhart, who was instrumental in building a 9,000-member church in Columbus, Ohio, from a small, struggling church, commented that he could do things in the thirtieth year of his ministry there that he never could have done in his twenty-ninth year.

One veteran pastor of small churches, Hal Camp, insists, "The first five years and the first 200 members are always the hardest."

Churches that grow are churches served not by pastors who view them as a stepping-stone to something better but by pastors who see potential and invest a major portion of their lives.

Most churches stop growing between 200 and 300 members because that is about all one pastor can handle. Peter Wagner says, "A one-person staff, with the help of a secretary, can handle a church up to about 350, or even larger if the church is not growing."[17] If a church wants to continue growing, it must plan ahead for expanded staff.

Growth Is Not Easy

When is a church too large? Roy Burkhart used to say that any church is too large that does not have opportunities for one-on-one relationships in groups of 20 or fewer.[18] The first congregation I served as a summer pastor had 90 people. By Burkhart's standards, it was too large. Roy Burkhart's congregation of 9,000 was not too large.

When my Panorama City church had grown from an average attendance of 12 to 20 to 40, one newcomer was troubled by what he felt were the resistant attitudes of the old-timers. I said to an old-timer, "If we're not careful, we may lose that family."

The reply was, "We need to think about how big we want to get, anyway. I'm not sure we want to get up around 250 again."

My response was, "The question now is, do we even want to be up around 40?"

The fear, I am convinced, is not fear of numbers.

The deeper fear is of change, of loss of control and power, of loss of the close-knit fellowship that survived harsh battles previously and wants to preserve that closeness.

One old-timer, commenting on the closing of ranks against a new person, reflected, "I've been a part of this church for 30 years. These are my best friends. We've been through everything together." And by implication, *We're not about to turn on each other*.

Turnaround Management talks about the need to "scan the horizon constantly for the first sign of a distress signal." These "signal flags are many and varied," say Rescue Management experts, and can include any one or more of the following: evidences of decline, sudden unwillingness to cooperate, overdrafts (this applies to churches, and we'll look at it later), significant marketing or product changes.[19]

Often the difference between growing, plateauing, or declining is a tightrope requiring great skill and maneuverability. It is an exciting, challenging, demanding task. I wouldn't do something else for the world.

I have discovered that in every church I have served, *everything worthwhile has been difficult to accomplish*. It always took more time and far more effort than I could have imagined. Murphy's Law applies:

"If anything can go wrong, it will."[20]

The corollaries also apply:

"Nothing is as easy as it looks.

"Everything takes longer than you think.

"Left to themselves, things tend to go from bad to worse.

"Whenever you set out to do something, something else must be done first.

"Every solution breeds new problems.

"Nature always sides with the hidden flaw."

Also, the quantization of Murphy's Law applies:

"Everything goes wrong all at once."

"And O'Toole's Commentary on Murphy's Law:

"Murphy was an optimist."

Vince Lombardi made a film which drums these principles into the heads of football players. The film is titled "Second Effort." It arouses players to do more than memorize plays and faithfully train and work hard. It urges them to keep going when everything within them would say "Stop," to pick up the extra necessary yards after they have been tackled.

Spinoza said:

"All things excellent
    are as difficult
        as they are rare."[21]

If good lives were simple, all people would be good. If great churches came with minimum effort, every church would be great. They aren't. They require the special gift to see those things that make for the greatness God intends, to take hold, and to never let go.

Vision. Doggedness. And that quality of tough love—staying, deep caring—that only God can give.

Teaching Helps for Chapter 5

Before the session:

☐ Arrange to have your special worship visitor be present for this session.

☐ Prepare these overhead transparencies: "Profile of a Pastor," "Profile of a Congregation," "No-Man's-Land," "Chaplain."

Suggested Lesson Plan

1. A judicatory executive from Idaho said, "The United Church of Christ is reestablishing what the United Church of Christ is, spelling it out in terminologies that the people can understand." Ask your group members to answer the following questions on paper:

"What is distinctive about my church?"

"What are the strengths of my denomination?"

Give each person three minutes. Use the kitchen timer. Then list some answers to each question on a chalkboard.

2. If you are the pastor, comment on the profile of the Church Growth pastor, using the transparency. Assess your personal strengths and weaknesses here. Share as frankly as the established trust level will

allow.

3. Show the "Profile of a Church Growth Congregation" transparency, and have each person write a sentence to describe your congregation in relation to each of these characteristics:

Loving:

Open:

Committed:

Flexible:

Willing to change:

Big in attitude:

4. At this point have your "mystery guest" share findings and impressions frankly and honestly. Let the group respond with questions and reactions. What do you learn that might be used to the betterment of the congregation?

5. Show "The No-Man's-Land" transparency. Discuss: "Is there a minefield between newcomers and old-timers in our church?"

"What are some of the quotes you have heard from newcomers?"

"Old-timers?"

"How can we move beyond that?"

6. Show the "Chaplain . . ." transparency. Ask each person to locate the minister on the line. Talk about how different groups in the congregation might perceive this differently.

7. Take a few minutes to let anyone share experiences with their prospect selected last week—strategies used, successes, failures.

The apostle Paul compared the excitement of sharing the Good News with an athlete who trains and sacrifices for a race. Read together I Corinthians 9:19-27. Then ask:

"Has sharing our faith cost us anything?"

"What has Paul to teach us?"

1. C. Peter Wagner, "The Cost of Church Growth," *Church Growth: America,* Volume 5, Number 5 (November—December 1979), p. 4 ff.

2. Lyle E. Schaller, *Survival Tactics in the Parish* (Nashville: Abingdon, 1977), p. 52 ff.

3. Write the Institute for American Church Growth, 150 S. Los Robles Ave., Suite 600, Pasadena, CA 91101. Or phone (800) 423-4844.

4. Available from the Institute for American Church Growth.

5. See the bibliography at the back. One excellent way to stay current is to become a member of the Church Growth Book Club. Write American Church Growth Book Club, 1705 Sierra Bonita Ave., Pasadena, CA 91104, or call (213) 798-0819.

6. Robert H. Schuller, *Your Church Has Real Possibilities* (Glendale, Calif.; Regal, 1974), pp. 72 ff.

7. Peter Wagner, "The Cost . . ." p. 13 ff.

8. Dean M. Kelley, *Why Conservative Churches Are Growing* (New York: Harper and Row, 1972), p. viii.

9. Joseph B. Mohr, *Call Chronicle,* Allentown, Penn., February 3, 1978.

10. Committee on Diminishing Membership, Church of the Brethren, 1980 report. Presentation with color overheads available from the Parish Ministries Commission, Evangelism Office, 1451 Dundee Avenue, Elgin, IL 60120.

11. Robert Leslie Hymers, *A Manual on How to Start House Churches* (unpublished), pp. 105-108.

12. Quoted on the "Toni Grant Show," radio KABC, January 21, 1981.

13. Lyle E. Schaller, *Hey, That's Our Church* (Nashville: Abingdon, 1975), p. 93 ff.

14. John M. Durkee and Ian B. Sharlit, "Ever Try Management by Rescue?" *American Banking Journal,* March 1980, p. 68.

15. Peter Wagner, *Your Church Can Grow: Seven Vital Signs of a Healthy Church* (Glendale, Calif.: Regal, 1976), pp. 55, 69.

16. Schaller, *Survival Tactics,* p. 27.

17. Wagner, "The Cost . . ." p. 10.

18. Some researchers now place the number at 50 to 100.

19. Durkee and Sharlit, "Ever Try . . ." p. 68.

20. Arthur Bloch, *Murphy's Law and Other Reasons Why Things Go Wrong* (Los Angeles: Price/Stern/Sloan, 1977).

21. Benedict Spinoza, *Ethics,* Part V. Prop. XLII, note.

PROFILE of a CHURCH GROWTH PASTOR

1. Hard worker
2. Always a student
3. Secure, not threatened
4. A person of vision
5. A person of faith
6. Disciplined
7. Very stubborn

PROFILE of a CHURCH GROWTH CONGREGATION

1. Loving
2. Open
3. Committed
4. Flexible
5. Willing to change
6. Big in attitude

THE NO-MAN'S-LAND

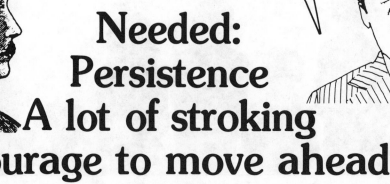

Old-Timers

"Who are all these new people in *our* church?"

"I'm not needed anymore."

"Nobody will ever take that job away from me!"

"If you don't do it my way, I'll leave."

Newcomers

"They want our money and our bodies but not our ideas."

"Maybe this isn't the church for us."

"We don't want to be a part of a one-family church."

"Don't they want new people?"

Needed:
Persistence
A lot of stroking
Courage to move ahead

CHAPLAIN
PASTOR
LEADER

- **Pay Dues**
- **Go to Meetings**
- **Bury dead/ Marry/Visit**
- **Wait!**

6 Sicknesses That Cripple & Kill

A few years back, Eda LeShan wrote a book entitled *The Wonderful Crisis of Middle Age*.[1] Many aspects of that book apply as directly to congregations as they do to people.

She tells in chapter six about going to see the movie *Love Story* with a middle-aged friend. "Erich Segal is a coward," the friend muttered as they walked out. "It's a real cop-out to kill off the young wife while they are still in the first blush of romance. It would have taken a lot more courage to let them live through marriage-in-middle-age."[2]

LeShan says that suddenly it dawns on us that we are 40 or 45 years old. We begin to take inventory of our lives as we never did before. Suddenly we realize that we will not read all the books we want to read or visit all the spots we want to visit. Life is limited. Time is running out.[3] We are not getting ready for something bigger and better. This is it. This is what life will be for us.

One woman with terminal cancer wept quietly when her doctor came into her hospital room. As he tried to reassure her, she interrupted him. "I'm not crying because I'm *dying*. I'm crying because I have never *lived*."[4]

However, middle age for congregations, as well as for people, can be a time of renewal, taking inventory, recharting courses, and beginning to live again. The years after age 30 or 40 or more can be the *best* years of a congregation's life. We realize who we are, what riches we possess. We find whole new reasons for being. Our lives become immersed without apology in the things that matter most. And a rebirth occurs.

As a person, I would not for the world return to the life of a teenager even if I could. Life is richer, fuller, happier, and less turbulent than it has ever been. Every year gets better. Every year I feel a greater challenge. "Aging," someone has said, "is the elegance of experience." It can be that way for churches, too.

Like an ecclesiastical version of TV's *Quincy* poring over the body of a victim for the cause of death or examining a sick person for symptoms, Peter Wagner diagnoses modern congregations. In his pioneering work, *Your Church Can Be Healthy*, he introduces the field of church pathology, identifying, naming, and analyzing some of the most common diseases that afflict the Body of Christ.[5]

"LET'S SEE NOW..."

Although the pathology of Church Growth is not included in most seminary or Bible school curricula of the past, it is an emerging field that is worthy of more than a passing awareness.

In that beginning work, Wagner listed eight illnesses. We will use his terms, except for one. And we will look at them as they especially apply to smaller congregations and to churches in middle age.

Terminal Illnesses

Church Growth experts have identified two illnesses that may prove to be terminal. Barring some special new discovery, death seems unpreventable.

The first is *ethnikitis*. Its presence was evident in a song in the controversial church musical "For Heaven's Sake" some 20 years ago:

A mighty fortress is our church,
A bulwark never failing,
Against the changing neighborhood,
Where sin is all-prevailing. . . .
If we let those outside in here,
They'll make the place a shambles.[6]

A Norwegian pastor tells about his home congregation in the Midwest, which once recorded in its annual report, "We have 94 souls and 8 Swedes." Such a congregation, drawing its life from its roots, its Old World heritage, when caught in a flood of another racial or ethnic group inevitably finds its young couples moving away. They may come back for a time. But when their children enter school, they look for a congregation nearer where they live. It is only a matter of time before that church will die. It has no base from which to draw. The kindest thing a pastor could do would be to help it die with dignity: to live out its remaining years with meaning and purpose, and perhaps to suggest that it leave some of its parts to others in a living testament, like an eye or kidney or heart donor. An example:

First Christian Church of Gardena, Calif., was serving a community that began to include blacks. The white families of the church accepted and welcomed the first blacks to arrive. But suddenly it all changed. Leapfrogging the blacks came wave after wave of Mexican-Americans, many speaking only Spanish.

My Anglo friend Hal Camp (who also spoke Spanish) pastored that church until the Hispanic membership reached 80 percent. In the latter months he shared the pastorate with a Spanish-speaking pastor of Mexican descent. When the new group was strong enough to survive, the remaining Anglo families started a new Anglo congregation at a distant point in the community, in Rowland Heights. The new community needed the kind of ministry to which they were accustomed and offered a base for solid growth.

The old church died. But it had the vision and graciousness to "will" enough of itself—its building, resources, leadership—so that a new life could emerge. Indeed, Jesus said it: "Unless a grain of wheat falls into the earth and dies, it remains alone" (Jn. 12:24, RSV).

Our purpose here is not to argue, as some would, that it need not be terminal. Faced with personal terminal illness, we all react at first by fighting its reality. Elisabeth Kubler-Ross in her wonderful book *On Death and Dying* describes that struggle so well. Sometimes people do beat the odds. But a good doctor accepts the gravity and reality of the situation and tries to help the patient realistically adjust to what is likely to be. And a wise family and responsible counselors try to help the person get beyond the stages of denial, anger, and bargaining to acceptance and adjustment to what will most probably be.

In the same manner, wise pastors will try to prepare congregations for the most realistic and meaningful adjustment to what the future may well hold. All the while, they know that no one can "play God" and state with certainty when and where death will occur.

A second illness identified as terminal is one Peter Wagner has called *old age*. I feel the term is misleading. *Populus Abandonmentosis* might describe it better. It is evidenced in the statement of one man from the rural Midwest who said, "Every year we grow more corn and less people."

Unlike ethnikitis, this is often a rural disease, although not always so. City churches may find their whole area being overtaken by miles of industry in every direction.

Robert Schuller in the excellent movie "How to Grow a Church" is asked the question "Can *any* church grow?"

His response is "*Yes*. Except, of course, in Death Valley and at the North Pole. You have to have people."[7]

However, a word of caution is necessary.

We can assume too easily that there is no growth potential.

The front page of the *Des Moines Register* on October 18, 1979, told of a town that "bursts with pride" over its "tiny church that refused to die." *Guideposts* magazine's Norman Vincent Peale Award, in fact, went to 43 members of the Hastings

57

United Methodist Church in Iowa. The turnaround came when they "started thinking about what they could do for the community." Before it was just a matter of wondering "how we could hang on and get the bills paid." They had actually closed their doors when a 45-year-old farmer-turned-pastor and a group known as the "Hastings Nine" refused to let it die.

The church steps were crumbling, the roof was leaking, the piano was out of tune. But they learned about people hospitalized in Omaha and went to visit them. They talked with a brokenhearted mother whose teenage son was an inmate in the state penal system. The farmer-turned-pastor went to visit the inmate and was instrumental in obtaining his parole. The membership began to increase. By Easter of 1978, about 90 people were at worship, a turnout not seen at that church in years. Bible study programs for adults emerged and a junior choir was organized.

Hastings United Methodist Church remains small, but on most Sundays attendance is three times what it was two years ago.

Their conclusion was that dwindling attendance, lack of funds, and an isolated location need not prove terminal "if concerned people, led by a concerned pastor, will just step out in faith to keep their church alive."

Some congregations must die. Some can be yoked or merged. Some need to develop a program within the limits of the resources available to them. For some, the disease goes into remission, and life is extended.

Other Illnesses

The six other illnesses listed by Wagner are not usually fatal.

1. *People blindness*. This is when we fail to see and respond to the cultural and ethnic richness around us. Chapter 8 will look at some possible responses to this illness.

2. *Hypercooperation*. When we are discouraged with a local setting, how easy it is to invest time in religious activities beyond the local church. Both pastors and lay people do this. They are very much like parents who "save the world" while neglecting their own children.

I spent 13 years in inner-city Harrisburg and was active in many interchurch and city-wide activities. At times I felt almost like a "minister to committees." I moderated a radio talk show on five area stations in central Pennsylvania. I pushed this cause and that.

When I left that church, I realized that *the only lasting thing was what I had done among my own people,* ministering to them, nurturing them, and training them to be ongoing members of the Body of Christ in that community. Everything else stopped when I stopped.

"My local church isn't all that great, so I invest my life in this or that or something else"—such an attitude will never foster growth. God's battle for the world comes down in most realistic terms to the local church. That's where the tire meets the road. If it can't happen there, it can't happen. Ecumania, big-name preachers, thrilling crusades—they come, they make their splash, they go.

Hypercooperation is a sickness, an escape from the hard tasks at hand. And it does not pay off.

3. *Koinonitis*. Koinonia is good. The New Testament talks about it. But fellowship and caring turned inward with a wall around it can go to seed. As the Arabs say, "All sunshine makes a desert."

A campfire ballad, "The Dummy Line," says:

There was a doctor by the name of Peck,
Fell down a well and he broke his neck.
Serves him right, as he should have known,
Should have tended to the sick and left the well alone.

As a girl growing up near Hershey, Penn., my wife attended a small rural Methodist church. During most of her childhood years, that congregation had about 20 people in attendance. The church was run by one family. They held most of the offices, chaired the committees, taught the classes, sang the solos, did most of the work.

During one brief period, another minister came and involved a wide range of people. For a few years the attendance shot up to nearly 100. Then he left, and family control returned. People left and the attendance went back down to 20.

Many of Jesus' followers were castoffs: a couple of unlettered fishermen, some tax collectors, some women with bad reputations—people with little schooling and even less religious training.[8] The growing edge of the churches I have served are often the castoffs—someone who was about to commit suicide but who was ministered to, some rejects from other situations, people lukewarm until a child got into deep trouble, people torn apart by divorce, a person who has failed: of such is the Kingdom built.

Wagner says the cure for koinonitis is to divide.[9] Start new groups. *A single-cell church will never grow.* A church where everyone does everything together will never grow.

When we started a choir again, some people objected that they were not invited to the choir Christmas party. They assumed that everybody went to everything.

Koinonitis—ingrown fellowship, an exclusiveness that locks others out—may be the chief debilitating illness of small churches.

4. *Sociological strangulation.* This is seen most often in two specific areas: (1) a church building that is too small, and (2) parking that is inadequate. Growing congregations are especially susceptible to this disease. Yogi Berra, former catcher for the New York Yankees, describes such a situation in his own inimitable way: ''Nobody goes there anymore; there are too many people.''

This can happen for small churches too. One small church in the Midwest is surrounded by cornfields, but the tiny parking lot is packed on Sundays. Growth for them is being strangled.

Schuller says if a church is to grow, it must have *surplus* parking![10]

Check it out. When the pillars of the church arrive, the lot may be half empty. No problem—for them! But take a careful look at five minutes past the time for the worship service to begin.

New people will drive around, see there is no parking, and leave. They may never even tell you they have come. They may never come back again.

And a sanctuary too full (what a thrill for the pastor) will shut off growth. When a sanctuary is 90 percent full, go to two services. ''But that will divide the church,'' the saints complain. Exactly! For as the church divides, new people with other friends and interests will gravitate. And although one of the services may seem terribly small, the total will be more than ever came to the single service.

To merge, to consolidate classes or groups or congregations (or denominations, studies show) is usually a sign of sickness. George Hunter says that to merge two churches is to end up with one congregation about the size of the larger of the two. The new math for church mergers is that one plus one does not equal two. One plus one equals about one and one-eighth. It is not the kind of mathematics that God enjoys.[11]

5. *Arrested spiritual development.* Those in small congregations tend to think of this disease as the exclusive ailment of large congregations. One critic of Church Growth confessed, ''I lived in a congregation that did not grow, and I knew why. We were in competition with a big church a few blocks away, and we couldn't put on its kind of razzle-dazzle program. But I maintain that in the Lord's eyes, we were healthier than that church.''[12]

We tend to label the big church as superficial. Numbers without deep commitment. Many people coming and going, but lacking in substantive quality.

I have served in both, and I know that small churches can be shallow, too. And some larger churches evidence great dedication. It is easy in a small congregation to focus on financial needs. The pastor's salary may absorb so much of the budget that little is left for adequate study materials or growth experiences. Bake sales, yard sales, petty gossip, narrow infighting, and long-standing feuds can become the routine menu.

Arrested spiritual development can sap the vitality of large and small alike.

6. *St. John's syndrome.* By this I mean the sickness talked about in those wonderfully revealing chapters at the outset of the Book of Revelation. In a time of extreme hardship and persecution, the Church was God's hope in that day. But the churches, some of them, had left their "first love," had grown "lukewarm," had become content and ineffective (Rev. 2: 4; 3: 16). It is the most common malady of the mid-life crisis of congregations. This disease can strike and cripple today.

Psychological Illnesses

We know that emotional and mental health affects our physical well-being as persons. Here are some examples of the same phenomenon among churches.

First, the problem of *memory.* Elizabeth Loftus of the University of Washington[13] relates the story of a man who remembered how as a very young boy he was kidnapped from his baby carriage. He could remember the horrified look on the face of his nurse, the expressions on the faces of his kidnappers. He could describe them and recall the events with amazing clarity, even though he had been quite young.

Only years later did the nurse confess that there had been no attackers, no kidnappers. She had taken the child. And what the man remembered was the story he had heard over and over.

People forget facts, says Elizabeth Loftus. They fabricate things to fill in the gaps between what they do remember accurately. They adjust their memory to suit their picture of the world.

Early childhood memories are dreamlike reconstructions of stories told by parents and friends. And many adult memories are as unreliable as the memories of children—encrusted with experiences, desires, and suggestions.

Churches do this. We think we recall the events that led us to this moment: the failure of a former pastor, the trauma around the departure of some key families, the reasons for the difficulties we now face.

But sometimes the fact is that we construct our memory to fit the feelings we now have. Those feelings are very real. But the legacy of the past we carry with us may not be rooted in reality.

Reality orientation is something personnel in convalescent centers are involved in with older people. Nurses and others must constantly help them recall today's date, *where* they are, *who* they are, *what in fact are the conditions* that surround them.

And churches need this.

A small-church study in the state of Washington revealed a whole set of false assumptions.[14]

The *assumption* was "Our church cannot accomplish much because we're all old." The *fact* was that only 12.5 percent of the area residents were over 65.

The *assumption* was "All the young married people have left our community." The *fact* was that 16.5 percent of the area residents were between 20 and 30 years of age.

The *assumption* was "There aren't many children around for our church school." The *fact* was that 37 percent of the area residents were between 0 and 19 years of age.

The *assumption* was "We're short on educated leadership." The *fact* was that 49.2 percent of the church membership had some college, a college degree, or postgraduate education.

The *assumption* was "We're poor. We can't afford the kind of church programs other areas can." The *fact* was that they were above average in income and wealth.

Research into the facts of a congregation's life can help it begin to see the reality of its situation. In the Washington state study, the conclusion was that "once the churches realized they had been programming with wrong assumptions, they began to ask who their members were, who were the people in the community that they ought to serve, and in a number of cases, *this alone* gave them new hope, new incentive, and new life."

Reality orientation—an important exercise for every congregation!

Inferiority complex is a term we all know. Every congregation has its own unique personality, mood, and flavor. And some are stunted because they are convinced they are inferior.

A wonderful pastor from the Christian church took a congregation without pay two years ago. His wife is a schoolteacher, and they lived on her salary at first.

When he came, there were 35 people. He looked out over that group and felt discouraged. Were there really the possibilities here for a living church? But as he looked, he realized that these were the people who had hung on, who had refused to leave when others faded into the woodwork. They were made of tough stuff.

The first Sunday there, they had a funeral service. They buried their past. He told them he never wanted to hear them refer to theirs as a "little church" ever again. They were *big*. Big in *faith*. Serving a big *God*. With a big *mission*.

They painted the church a different color to give it new visibility. They began immediately to institute some things that gave evidence of life.

Music is a key to a growing church, he felt, but they had no choir. So he began to bring in musical groups. At first he and his wife paid for the groups out of their own pockets.

If a *church* is to grow, *people* must grow in faith and in confidence. He began to use them in leadership roles, to encourage them, to praise them. He took them with him into the pulpit to share in worship leadership. He would say, "In a year, I expect you to take this job."

At the end of the first six months, the church began to pay a small part of his salary—$45 a week. They paid more at the end of the first year, more after 18 months, and still more after two years.

People wanted a youth director, but the pastor knew that a youth program is not the key to initial growth. An earlier priority was to begin to find and train church school teachers.

They had no young couples, so he developed a wedding package—counseling, psychological testing, the wedding service, music, a tape of the service, a picture of the couple in front of the bulletin board with their names and the date on it—all for a fee competitive with other churches and wedding chapels. They advertised in the Yellow Pages.

In the first two years they had 50 weddings. Six of those couples came into the church. Three other couples from other communities eventually united with churches in their own areas. There are the beginnings of a young-married class.

When a congregation feels inferior, not good enough to invite their own best friends, ashamed of who they are, no growth can occur.

Depression afflicts some churches. Counselors sometimes describe this as anger turned inward. Churches are sometimes filled with lingering anger about the past. Churches too long on denominational support can have a welfare complex, which makes them dependent and angry. Some bad scene from the past can poison today.

Angers need to be looked at, gotten to the surface, dealt with, and resolved, or a church will be forever enslaved to its own restricting attitudes.

Narcissism, egotism, being in love with themselves can arrest growth. One judicatory official lamented the number of people in his church who don't feel good enough about themselves to reach out. Then he went on to say that those who do feel good about themselves often don't want anyone strange coming in to mess up what they have.

So in love with themselves are some that they have lost sight of a greater and more wondrous love, the love of God for His hurting, lost people.

Schizophrenia is found in some settings—a loss of contact with reality, a disintegration of personality, a flying-apartism. So torn with dissension are some groups that they need a major miracle of healing before they can ever be "together" enough to grasp the mission to which they have been called.

Some are almost *catatonic* in their state, like the extreme mental patient who sits or stands staring off into space, totally separated from reality. Some churches are in the world but don't even know it. Theirs is a realm totally cut off. They may be bound for Heaven, but they are of little earthly good.

And among some there is *projection*, a desire to lay the faults within them, the condition of their being, on someone else.

We could go on. The point is that many of the psychological ills that beset individuals also beset congregations.

But there is One who can bring healing. Many times the Great Physician turns us outward, away from focusing on the sickness to rediscover a purpose bigger than ourselves—a purpose so big that it consumes us, calls forth all our energies, and hurls us down paths so exciting that our mental and emotional crutches are left behind and we don't even miss them.

The Christ who gave a beggar new sight can restore vision to His Church. The Jesus who helped the lame to walk again can teach His people today how to walk responsibly through His world. The Nazarene who helped people to love and trust and reach out in the first century can and will do that for us, too, when we are ready.

Teaching Helps for Chapter 6

Before the class session:

☐ Prepare the overhead transparency on "Diseases of Churches."

☐ Get a water-soluble marking pen for writing on transparencies. Immediately following the session, use damp facial tissue to clean; do not leave markings on too long, or they work into the transparency.

☐ Prepare copies of Medical Chart 8, one for each group member.

Suggested Lesson Plan

1. Look together at the transparency on "Diseases." One by one, share the author's description regarding each disease. Together decide with regard to each disease whether it applies to your situation: "not at all," "perhaps," or "for sure."

Then come back and look at those that apply "for sure." Can you agree on what must be done?

I once stood in the hallway outside the room of a church member who had just had a heart attack. I listened in amazement as three doctors disagreed on the nature and severity of what had happened and therefore were in sharp disagreement on what ought to be done.

On what can you agree if your congregation is to move from sickness to health? Together list some specific steps to be taken.

Possible questions for discussion:

"If you were to die tomorrow (and you will in some tomorrow), who have you brought into the life of the congregation to replace you in terms of service to the group? What if you *couldn't* leave until you had trained your replacement?

"What is the primary ethnic group in our congregation? Do we suffer from ethnikitis?

"Does populus abandonmentosis affect the life in our congregation? Has our membership kept pace with the population in our area, or have we abandoned the people in favor of the status quo? How can we find out the needs of the new population in our area?

"What ten things do we wish children and new converts to know after instruction in our church school/membership class?" (If you do not know—perhaps you should enroll!)

2. Ask each person to write a sentence about each of these psychological ills as it may apply to your congregation:

Memory:
Reality orientation:
Inferiority complex:
Depression:
Narcissism:
Schizophrenia:
Catatonic:
Projection:

Then share what you have written. Discuss ways to work at those that apply to your church. Are the illnesses serious enough to seek outside help?

3. Read together Romans 12:4, 5. Each church is more than a collection of people. It is a living organism with its own characteristics and personality.

It has habits and attitudes all its own.

Hand out Medical Chart 8. Psychologists use drawings to get at feelings which may not be easily put into words. *Ask each person in your group to draw* your congregation as he or she sees it. You may want to use human features. You may want to use the head or body (or both) of one or more animals. How do you see your congregation?

Then share what you have drawn with others.

Discuss your feelings.

4. Take a few minutes to share more progress with your individual prospects. Also report on progress within the congregation at moving to put to use ideas looked at in previous chapters.

5. Offer sentence prayers expressing your hopes, disappointments, and, above all, your responses to what God wants your congregation to be.

1. Eda LeShan, *The Wonderful Crisis of Middle Age* (New York: Warner, 1974).
2. LeShan, *The Wonderful Crisis,* p. 143.
3. LeShan, p. 18.
4. LeShan, p. 19.
5. C. Peter Wagner, *Your Church Can Be Healthy* (Nashville: Abingdon, 1979).
6. Lyrics by Helen Kromer, "For Heaven's Sake" (New York: Christian Society for Drama, 1961).
7. The first film produced by the Institute for American Church Growth. It is well worth showing to a congregation more than once.
8. See I Corinthians 1, especially verse 26.
9. C. Peter Wagner, op. cit., p. 87.
10. Robert Schuller, *Your Church Has Real Possibilities* (Glendale, Calif.: Regal, 1974).
11. In an Advanced Growth Seminar sponsored by the Institute for American Church Growth, at Pasadena, Calif., January, 1981.
12. Vernard Eller, in forum with Peter Wagner, John Huffman, Larry Dewitt, Ben Patterson, "Must a Healthy Church Be a Growing Church?" *Leadership* magazine, Winter Quarter 1981, p. 129.
13. *Time* Magazine, January 5, 1981, p. 89.
14. David J. Brown, *Washington Small-Church Project* (12 North Chelan, Wenatchee, WA 98801), p. 9.

DISEASES of CHURCHES

DISEASES THAT KILL	APPLIES TO US . . .	Not At All	Perhaps	For Sure	Prescription
	ETHNIKITIS				
	POPULUS ABANDONMENTOSIS				
Others That Cripple	PEOPLE BLINDNESS				
	HYPER-COOPERATION				
	KOINONITIS				
	SOCIOLOGICAL STRANGULATION				
	ARRESTED SPIRITUAL DEVELOPMENT				
	ST. JOHN'S SYNDROME				

Medical Chart 8
A Portrait of My Congregation

On this page, draw you congregation as you see it.
How do you see your congregation?

7 Closing the Back Door

Some denominational executives awhile back got the idea of raising their benevolence budgets by suggesting (or assessing) "per member amounts." For every member, congregations would give so many dollars for the denomination, so many for the judicatory, so many for camps and colleges and seminaries and retirement homes.

Some congregations, to beat the game, immediately looked for inactive members to prune from the rolls, so that outreach obligations would not be so burdensome.[1] Some larger congregations would think nothing of writing off several hundred inactive members in one fell swoop.

Actually, all churches have members who go through periods of inactivity or loss of interest.

For the small church, this can be disastrous. The loss of one or two families through discouragement or disagreement can put the entire operation in a tailspin.

We tend to blame the inactives for their condition. Their ardor has cooled. We pray for them, preach against them, even visit them—often with little return for our heroic effort.

It may come as a surprise to realize in the Parable of the Coin in Luke 15, the coin was lost not through its own neglect but because of the woman's. "I have found the piece which *I had lost*," she announced (vs. 9).

A former United Methodist pastor, John (Tim) Savage, insists that a high percentage of our inactives are reclaimable, many with *one visit*. The Disciples of Christ have used him widely in workshops under the title "Reunion." His L.E.A.D. consultants have much to teach us.

Savage, enriched by theological training, his own pastoral experience, and considerable psychological background, has some important things to tell us.

Anxiety-Provoking Events

One is his discovery that 95 percent of all inactives started down the road of inactivity because of "*an anxiety-provoking event.*" Something happened to jolt them or hurt them or turn them away.[3]

He lists the causes as: (1) pastor, (2) church member, (3) family member, or (4) overwork.

His studies used to show that the pastor was the usual culprit. More studies have revealed that the underlying causes are often directly related to interaction with another *family member*. Sometimes a husband and wife have tensions going. Sometimes one will use the church—either by excessive activity or by inactivity—to "get at" the other.

Others are just plain tired out. Church has demanded too much for too long. They turn away for some breathing space.

One woman said to me, "You pastors can change churches when you get tired and discouraged. I've been in this one for 20 years. I think I need some change."

Savage lists four kinds of events that can cause a person to become inactive: (1) reality, (2) moral, (3) neurotic, and (4) existential.

Some shattering events are rooted in *reality*. A church school teacher is not asked to continue. The pastor is overheard to say, "We don't need any more of that," referring to the best effort of a faithful member. Toes are stepped on, fur rubbed the wrong way, people offended.

Sometimes the problem is *moral*. Presbyterians still remember Angela Davis. Episcopalians feel themselves being torn apart over the debate to ordain admitted homosexuals. The Vietnam War, abortion, civil rights: many are the moral issues that have caused members to question their continued participation in a congregation if they find themselves at odds with the denomination or pastor, church school teacher or congregation.

Tim Savage tells of a sermon that was strong against abortion. In the weeks that followed, a leading family in that church began to attend less frequently. Eventually they dropped out altogether.

The pastor went to visit them and expressed concern at their absence. Their response was noncommittal. Church just didn't mean as much anymore, they said. Some of their former interest wasn't there just now. Maybe they needed "a break from things."

Unknown to the pastor, the family's teenage daughter had become pregnant. In the stress and hurt of that event, the family, without talking to anyone else, had decided the best course was an abortion. The pastor was simply fulfilling his obligation to preach the Word of God as he understood it. But in so doing, a hurting family felt shut off. They also felt too hurt, too ashamed even to talk to him about it.

Every great moral issue is a great moral issue because people are divided in their views about it. If they were not divided, it would not be an issue. And confronted with every such issue, pastors feel two claims: first, to faithfully preach the will of God as they best understand it, and, secondly, to pastor hurting, uncertain people at the same time.

During the Vietnam War, how could a minister who felt it was immoral speak against it with force when seated in his congregation were the families and friends of soldiers dying in that war?

There is no easy answer. We need *great courage* and *great compassion,* both in large doses, at the same time.

Sometimes the anxiety-provoking incident, on the other hand, has nothing to do with moral issues. It is simply *neurotic* in nature. How many times have people thundered at me, ''My wife was in the hospital for three weeks and you didn't go and visit her!''

And I respond, ''I didn't know your wife was in the hospital. No one told me.''

And the person responds, ''You're our pastor. It's your business to know.''

That is neurotic.

Even in church, people imagine hurts and slights that to them are very real but are not rooted in reality.

A fourth reason is *existential.* We're growing older, for example. We realize we don't have forever. Some react by wanting to throw off every vestige of the past and be free, *totally free,* to do their own thing, to make of life what they can while life lasts.

John Savage has also helped in this area by outlining a ''dropout track.'' Basically he is saying that after every anxiety-provoking event there is often *anger.* We've all had this. Something goes wrong;

someone says something wrong; sometimes *we* mess up.

I remember one time before a packed college church—more than 600 people—when I had memorized a poem to use as the closing prayer. I planned to deliver it down front without any notes. Some critical people were there, and I wanted that service to be as near perfect as possible. It went well up to the end. But in those closing, dramatic moments, I could not for the life of me remember a *word* of that poem. I felt like an utter fool as I muttered some meaningless sentences impromptu.

If just one person you respect cares enough to say, ''It's sure good to know that you're human, too,'' it can make all the difference in the world.

Often when we feel angry, hurt, cut off, a simple thing like a smile, a wink, a warm hand on the shoulder, or some small expression of caring can take away the sting. Suddenly the anxiety-provoking event is back in perspective, and we are ready to put it aside and go on.

But if there is no such warmth or awareness, we may tuck our anger inside, where it sticks in us and begins to fester.

After-church fellowship times are good opportunities to observe people. A sensitive congregation will notice if Bill is not smiling today, if Sarah has wiped a tear from the corner of her eye, if the Joneses rush off, if the Franklin family has been absent for two weeks in a row.

If the hurt is not seen and resolved, a change is likely to be seen in giving patterns and attendance patterns. Whereas a family may have been present three Sundays out of four, that may drop to two Sundays out of four, or one Sunday out of four. Then they are not there at all.

Turtles and Skunks

Savage says all of us are either turtles or skunks. Turtles tend to take the blame on themselves, to express the feeling that they are no good or inadequate. ''It's all my fault. I'm just not a good teacher.''

Skunks tend to spray their anger all over everyone else. "What's the matter with them? They're a bunch of blockheads. If that pastor had half a brain, we wouldn't be in this mess."

And the observation is that among studies of inactive church members, in almost every instance, *turtles are married to skunks*. You might check that out among your married friends.

Sealing Off the Church

As the anger settles in, behavior changes. People are unable to speak very clearly about what they believe.

They drop out. And most inactives go through *a period of six to eight weeks of waiting*. They are holding back to see if *any*one will phone them or visit them.

I talked with a church secretary heavily involved in her church. Her entire family is deeply dedicated. They went on a six-week vacation. There had been no anxiety-provoking event for them. They had simply been away on extended travels. But when they returned, not one person at the church said, "We missed you" or "Where were you?" This lifelong member of the denomination—the church secretary, no less—said she felt like never going back if no one cared for them any more than that.

How much more do the hurting people who have dropped out eagerly wait to see if anyone cares? A caring church will not let anyone be away without noticing their absence and seeing that someone is at their home to visit.

Sometimes we know they are hurting but hold back. One couple fairly new to our church came regularly. He was Roman Catholic and still attended mass at times. One Sunday she was in church by herself and said they had separated. I made a few attempts to phone him but never got through. I stopped by a few evenings at suppertime, several times later in the evening, hoping I might find him. Yet I did not go at it as if it had been one of my own immediate family. Why?

The truth is, we *all* hurt. We all carry pain. And most of us have enough pain of our own without wanting to take on the pain and hurt of others.

Tragedy comes into other lives, and unless people are very close to us, we feel for them, we genuinely hurt for them, but we do not relish the thought of going to them and letting them pour out their hurt to us. It seems almost more than we can bear.

So the wife, who had the courage to keep coming, still comes to our church. The husband, whom none of us cared about deeply enough to persist in our efforts to risk sharing his pain, went back to his Catholic church.

With most dropouts there is a waiting period of six to eight weeks. If there is no response from the church, at the end of that period they *seal off the church emotionally and begin to reinvest their lives* in other ways.

It may be in another church. But at least half the time it is in *some other activity*. They begin to devote the time and money they had given to the church to a cabin or a camper. Or they become active in a lodge or club. They take up some new hobby that consumes them.

They do not simply stay home and sulk. Their lives are given over to something else.

Dropping inactive members from the rolls, however gently, is probably the worst thing we can do if we ever hope to see them in church again.

One extremely active man in a church I served shared, during a discussion about dropping inactives, how there had been a period when things in his life had not been going well. His business was in trouble, his marriage was shaky, and he dropped out of church completely. He said that if the church had dropped him at that time, he never would have come back. But people were patient and loving, and one day he realized what he was missing. At a receptive period in his life, he returned.

That story could be told by many people.

The Washington state study of small congregations suggested that the inactive list is the *least* profitable place to recruit. It suggested that congregations trade inactive lists! Inactives have emotional entanglements that make it difficult to work back to a warm, involved relationship with their former congregation, that study suggested.

That is one answer.

Listening Skills

John Savage suggests a better answer: the development of *listening skills* among a core group in your congregation, helping members to be able to really hear what people are saying.

The development of these skills requires a workshop experience. They need to be understood and practiced and refined.

Some of the things Savage works at include:

Recognizing *"screening"*—the ways we shut others out. A woman with important ties to the community began to attend a church and to sing in the choir. Some felt she did not have the best voice, to put it mildly. You could actually see choir members who sat next to her turning their backs to her.

As you survey fellowship activities, you can see new people, eager to be welcomed, making their rounds of the little groups of people talking. Stand and watch sometime, and see if they are taken into any of these groups. In some friendly churches, people are so deep into their own fellowships that they scarcely notice the newcomer. Does the person receive more than a "Hello" and "What's your name?" and "It's so good to have you here"?

A simple exercise is to have two or three people engage in conversation. Then take a forward person and tell him to try to get into the group discussion. Let everyone know that the task of the group is to keep him out, even if it means turning backs on him. He is not to be permitted to share in their discussion, no matter what.

People will laugh. But it may be a nervous laugh. For this happens many times.

Using lag time. We speak at the rate of 100 to 150 words a minute. But we can process about 400 to 500 words a minute. The time left over is called lag time.

Often as we talk, we are so intent on formulating what we want to say next that we scarcely hear what the other person is saying. A good listener uses that extra time, the lag time, to try to really *hear*. What is the person really saying?

Paraphrasing. An important tool is to make sure you understand by saying, "Are you saying such and such?" It is a simple device you can have your people practice one-on-one.

Checking perceptions. Along with this, it is helpful to make sure you are sensing feelings correctly. "I have the impression this makes you very angry." If they say the pastor is a lazy bum, you may respond by saying, "You seem to feel rejected because Pastor Jones has failed you in your time of need." *Naming* the emotions you sense in the other person can help that person and yourself.

Fogging. The Scriptures suggest that a soft answer turns away wrath. When someone hurls out an acid-filled comment, one way to respond is to listen carefully and then reply by giving back *the truth of that statement.*

"The church school lesson today was terrible."
Possible response: "Frank didn't seem very well prepared today."

"The pastor hasn't been to see us in over a year. He's got to be the laziest pastor we've ever had."
Possible response: "I agree, pastoral visitation on a regular basis is not one of his strongest points." The purpose is not to feed the anger but to dispel it by letting the person know you hear and understand.

We have done this with angry teenagers in our home, and it can work wonders. After a half-dozen times at fogging, they usually settle down and talk quite sensibly.

"You never let us do anything."
Response: "True, we are more strict than some parents."

"Some parents! You wouldn't even let us go to the party after the ball game. You aren't too smart."
Response: "We do have a lot to learn."

"An awful lot."
Response: "I agree, an *awful* lot."

You never try to feed in the *correct* information. You do not try to argue or set them straight. But neither do you add to misconceptions. You simply affirm the truth in whatever they say, if that is possible. Probably no other skill helps so much to diffuse anger.

Listening for stories. As we talk, we tell stories. Sometimes it is only a sentence. But it gives clues into the turmoil that may be in our hearts.

A person may say one thing with his words but quite another by the stories he tells. The first story often gives a clue to what subsequent stories will reveal.

A man I scarcely knew said to me, "If I were going to hold up a supermarket, I wouldn't wear a mask. I'd just go in. Short people would say I was tall. Tall people would say I was short."

Only later did I discover that some of the stories he told me gave clues into his own past and struggles.

Another man talked glowingly of what Jesus had done in his life. He was a dry alcoholic. His wife, a devoted Christian, had helped him turn things around. He recounted the warmth and security there. But as he talked, he mentioned at one point that he would never forgive himself if anything happened to his wife or child. There were repeated images of violence in what he said. Later I suggested to a psychologist who had also heard the man's stories, "It sounds as though he is struggling with uncontrollable anger in his life, an anger that frightens him." The psychologist agreed.

More of us need to enter this wonderful world of listening. Since sharing in one of Savage's workshops, I have flown on planes across the country and by simply hearing well what seatmates were saying, they have commented, "I've told you things today I have never told anyone."

Sometimes, after sharing deeply, a person may feel ashamed. If he has said more than he intended, you may need to reassure him that everything is still okay. And you must never share his confidence with anyone.

As We Visit

When we go to visit someone who has dropped out, or when we relate to someone hurting, there are at least two temptations. One is to take literally what they say. A person may say, "I hate them; I hate them all." What he means may be, "Doesn't anyone there care about me?"

The other is to try immediately to solve problems. Someone says the choir director picks the wrong anthems. Immediately we suggest that he go talk to the choir director. Chances are that is not the real problem at all.

Every hurting person must be allowed to talk long enough to feel confident that he can talk freely to us and we will listen. He must also feel that he can trust us with what he says.

Congregations that want to close the back door would do well to share in a workshop on inactives. Short of that, they can gain exposure to listening skills from others who work at that. Parent Effectiveness Training[4] stresses the same thing with regard to parent-child relationships. But the skills apply universally.

Concluding the Visit

Critical to every visit to inactives is being able to bring it to a successful conclusion. Salespeople call this "closure." We will look further at techniques for closure in chapter 10 as we talk about sharing our faith.

Savage suggests six types of closure with inactives:

1. Negotiate with them to return.

2. Negotiate a second or third visit. This is often necessary if they have been away very long.

3. Negotiate termination. This is the last resort. Savage suggests you drop someone from membership only after four, five, six, or seven calls.

4. No movement. They may indicate they want to remain members but are not ready or able to move in any direction right now.

5. Transfer letters to another congregation.

6. Referral to another professional.

The most important thing you bring to this experience are your own feelings of love. Ninety percent of the people visited, insists Savage, are quite negotiable when they have a caring person with them.

Here are some specific questions that are helpful for closure with inactives. These come only after much listening.

"What would be most helpful now?"

"Help me understand your expectations of the church."

"What needs to be different?"

"What are the feelings you think you will have if you walk up the sidewalk of the church?"

One of the most frequent excuses for inactivity is, "I was forced to go to church as a child."

Savage suggests the following kind of response: "Sounds like that's a commandment your folks laid on you. How long have you been breaking that commandment?" Following their answer, "Seems like you've broken it long enough to lay off it." Or, "How long do you need to break it to feel liberated?"

Help the people find their own way through their hesitation and resistance.

The most successful closures are when the inactives themselves suggest a solution. You are miles ahead if they can be given time and encouragement to suggest their own way back.

Plenty of patience, active listening, and genuine caring can work miracles.

The Initial Contract

But the best way to minimize inactivity among our church members is at the point when people first enter the church, long before any anxiety-provoking event occurs. With what understandings do they come? With what kind of "contract"?

Near the end of every inquirers' class, I ask prospective members to write on one side of a piece of paper what they want and expect from the church. On the other side I have them write what the church can expect from them. We talk about their answers.

Some people come in saying they want to be a part of a church where there is no fighting, no disagreements. I need to say, "That won't be true here. We do disagree. Sometimes strongly. I hope we disagree in a helpful, not a destructive way."

All Long-Term Relationships

It is helpful to know that *all long-term relationships go through certain phases*. These are *predictable*. And there is *no way to stop them*. Whether marriage or job or church, some predictable things happen.

Gathering data and *developing expectations* is the first phase of every long-term relationship. The young man and young woman date, get to know each other. The potential employee is interviewed, and the two sides ask each other many questions. The would-be member may attend a series of classes, or sit with a pastor, or question a friend for hours about what is involved.

Then comes *commitment*. Marriage. Signing the job contract. Being received into the membership of the church.

A period of *stability and productivity* follows. The honeymoon. Dedicated service at the job. Committed activity in a church.

But, because of the very nature of life, hard things come. The wife says, "When you said you wanted children, I had no idea you meant seven." Or the husband says, "Why is this house always a mess?"

Disruption is a part of any long-term relationship. It comes to us all.

And the possibilities that follow are:
1. *Termination*
2. *Return to the initial commitment*
3. *Renegotiation*

Many in our world move easily toward *termination*. At many jobs, the turnover rate is very high. People would rather move on than struggle to make the necessary adjustments. Divorce is increasingly common. And many unhappy church people say, "Hey, why fight it? I'll go to a church where I can slip in and attend without all this hassle."

Some, perhaps painfully and reluctantly, go the route of *recommitment*. "I was wrong." Or, "I wasn't wrong, but it means enough that I will go back to what I promised and suffer through."

But by far the most positive response is *renegotiation*. Healthy groups are always in the process of renegotiation. Healthy relationships are formed knowing that along the way we change and situations change and new understandings will need to be arrived at. The wife is working full-time now, so the husband agrees to get the evening meal and help with the cleaning. The job has grown so much that the worker agrees to work some overtime for the next few weeks while a new person can be hired and trained. The church member who is bone-tired is granted a leave from all pestering to take on jobs. He or she agrees to come regularly but is on a sabbatical from tasks.

I know a young Protestant woman married to a Roman Catholic. Their contract with their pastor was that they each wanted to share in the other's religion. They would be absent from her church for some blocks of time to fulfill their obligations to the husband's faith. They would each take some responsibilities, but not as many as if both belonged there. They expected to be able to give themselves fully in the time available. They expected to be able to do this without being pressured into some other pattern.

Healthy churches know that disruptions come in all long-term relationships and build into their program opportunities for personal renegotiation.

Folding New Members

Win Arn has said that within one year every new member is one of three things. He or she is either (1) a member of some group, or (2) serving on some board or committee, or (3) he has become inactive.

A United Church of Christ pastor friend shared *six steps for folding new members into the life of the church*. Following these six steps can do much to diminish inactivity.

1. *Within 24 hours:* the lay leader of the congregation visits the newly received member, welcoming him and taking an interest and talent inventory.

2. *Within one week:* the new member's sponsors call. These sponsors stay with him for six months. If he is not in church, they call to discover why.

3. *Within one month:* the new member participates in some work or fellowship activity. Pictures of all new families with their names are posted on the bulletin board.

4. *Within three months:* a stewardship team calls to receive his financial pledge.

5. *Within six months:* the new member is named to some board or committee in the church.

6. *After six months:* the individual or couple becomes sponsors for another new person or family.[5]

A booming church not far from where I live hired a super minister of visitation evangelism. He was the kind of fellow who could spend an hour or so in a home and, by the time he left, have the people committed to joining the church he represented. Every Sunday new members paraded up front. In two years he alone brought in 420 members.

But a year later the church had lost as many members.

What does it profit a church that has a wide-open front door and takes in many members, if the back door is open even wider, and the new members gained are soon lost?[6]

A congregation serious about growing learns how to close its back door.

Teaching Helps for Chapter 7

Before the class session:

☐ Have seating that can be moved into small clusters.

☐ Prepare these overhead transparencies: "Savage's 'Dropout Track' " and "All Long-Term Relationships."

Suggested Lesson Plan

1. In your own words, present or review together John Savage's "Dropout Track" using the overhead. Share examples of the four kinds of anxiety-provoking events: reality, moral, neurotic, and existential. Have any of them been true in your congregation?

2. Practice some of the listening skills.

Screening. Use the exercise suggested in the text, where two or three people engage in conversation while someone attempts to break into the group, but the others will not allow that.

Lag time and paraphrase. Divide the group into pairs. Have one person say not more than five sentences about something he cares about. Ask the other person to repeat what he heard the first person saying. The first person is to check to make certain that all that was said is there. Then reverse the process: not more than five sentences, followed by repeating. Give each person four or five times to talk and then four or five to respond. (This is a helpful exercise for husband and wife, parent and child, teacher and student, employer and employee, etc.)

Perception check. This is fun to practice. Let a couple do it. Let one share some genuine problem, and let the other respond by noting the feelings expressed. Let them work at it for five minutes or as long as it is going well. Talk about what has happened after they are finished.

Then try it one-on-one throughout the whole group.

Fogging. Use three people: one to express genuine anger, a second to repeat back the *truth* of what is said, and a third to observe. Give them three minutes. Then let the observer stop and evaluate what has happened. Change roles so each person in the trio does each thing.

Storytelling. Combine groups of three into groups of six, with chairs in a circle. Let one person talk about some important area of life. Listen for stories, descriptive words, phrases. Are stories being told about hurt, hope, fears, faith?

Using all the skills. In groups of six, let one person share thoughts in an area he cares deeply about. Assign one person to listen and respond, using all of the above skills. Let the others in the group observe. After ten minutes, let the observers share what they saw happening. How well did the listener pick up on clues? Were significant things said that the listener missed?

Then let another person talk and another listen, until all have participated.

3. Look together at the "All Long-Term Relationships" transparency. Where could your congrega-tion strengthen its relationship to members? Where is it weak?

At the point of entrance?

At the point of dedication—not using it adequately?

At the point of hurt?

At the point of being able to renegotiate?

"How would you feel about having your name dropped from your family roll if you had not attended the family reunion for two years?"

"What do you expect from the church? What can the church expect from you?" List these answers on the opposite sides of a plain piece of paper. Collect. Read them to group after shuffling.

Looking at Arn's analysis of new members, list new members in your church in the last year. Are new members in category 1, 2, or 3? Does your church assign sponsors?

Talk about where and how your congregation might strengthen its life together. Are there persons willing and qualified to work at a ministry to inactives? It is difficult, demanding work. They will need to visit after a person has been away for no more than four weeks. They need to come together for assignments, sharing, mutual strengthening.

Check with your denomination or contact L.E.A.D. Associates directly to learn of a workshop in your area. Have as many people as possible, including the pastor, participate. The church may want to pay part, the participants part.

4. Look together at the six steps for folding new members into the life of the church. Is that usable for your congregation? How might you adapt it to your needs?

5. Ask everyone to write a note to one of your new members now! Take five minutes. Tell the new member how much you appreciate his role in church life and ask how you can assist growth.

6. Share successes and failures in working with your prospects. Continue to update the group on ideas implemented in the congregation.

7. Look at Luke 15: 8-32 together. Talk about the elements in each story. What do they say about lostness, about turning again, about receiving back?

"Do we make it difficult for people who have been away to come back? Will it be difficult to walk through those doors again? What kind of greeting do they get?"

8. In your closing prayers, name some members who need the church but are separated from it. Ask for guidance, love, understanding, and above all, the gift of listening.

1. A better way is to ask congregations to consider a certain percentage of their total budget for benevolences.

2. Information available from Agency for Religious Leadership Education and Development, P. O. Box 311, Pittsford, NY 14534. Phone (716) 586-8366.

3. See John Savage, *The Apathetic and Bored Church Member* (Pittsford, N.Y.: L.E.A.D. Consultants, 1976).

4. D. Thomas Gordon, *P.E.T.–Parent Effectiveness Training* (New York: Plume, 1970)—one source for learning about listening skills.

5. Shared by Lewis Knight, adapted from a plan developed by the First Community Church of Dallas, Texas. See also Lyle E. Schaller, *Assimilating New Members* (Nashville: Abingdon, 1978).

6. An accompanying problem is that of nonresident members. *One-third* of the Southern Baptist membership, for example, is nonresident. If the larger Church is to be vital, how important for congregations to let go of people who move away and actively work to involve them in a living relationship with the Body where they live.

SAVAGE'S "DROPOUT TRACT"

Anxiety-provoking event

Rooted in	Related to
Reality	Family member
Moral	Pastor
Neurotic	Church member
Existential	Overwork

↓

Anger

↓

Verbal messages

↓

Change in behavior
(less worship, giving, faith)

Dropout line

↓

Waiting period—6 to 8 weeks

↓

Reinvestment in other activities

↓

50% not in church

All Long-Term Relationships go through phases. These are predictable, and there is no way to stop them.

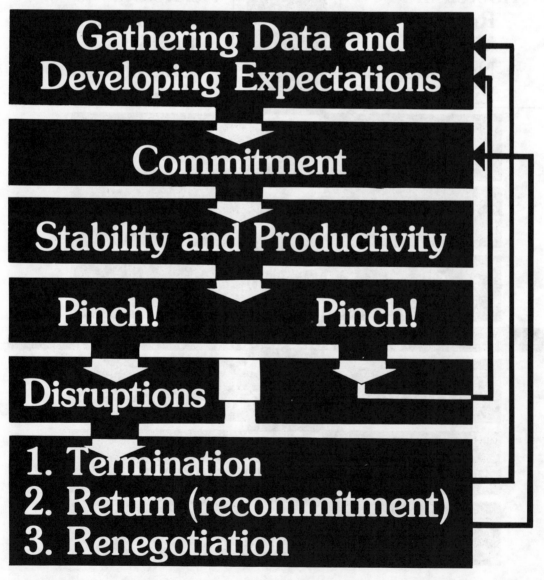

Gathering Data and Developing Expectations

↓

Commitment

↓

Stability and Productivity

↓

Pinch!   Pinch!

Disruptions

1. Termination
2. Return (recommitment)
3. Renegotiation

8 Developing a Many-Sided Evangelism

In the arithmetic of God, churches multiply by dividing. We have already noted that a single-celled congregation does not grow. People need more than one basic group to take hold of and relate to. As the number of groups increase, the possibilities for people to relate and be tied into the program also increase.

Many congregations have a one-sided ministry. They may be, for example, a "family church" . . . perhaps middle-class, old-fashioned values, parents and children together in worship, family night fellowship activities—they keep the traditional home strong.

That is not an unworthy type of ministry.

However, 41 percent of the community in which I live is *single*: It is made up of never married, or divorced, or widowed people. Many of them will remain single. They feel cut off, shut out.

In our community are also *Koreans*. Many do not speak English. They eat Korean food. They observe Korean customs.

There are also *Vietnamese*. They, too, feel cut off. They want to be with people who speak their language and share their history and customs.

Many *Mexican-Americans* live among us. Many expect someday to return to Mexico. Many speak Spanish. They prefer their foods; they cherish their celebrations.

There are *Cubans* who also speak Spanish. But they feel no ties to Mexicans. Their foods, hopes, politics, and expectations are very different.

Some members are *geographically distant* from our church. They are close friends, but travel time prevents them from full participation.

There are *deaf* people in our community. They feel alienated from the church. They feel uncomfortable in crowds of hearing people.

The truth is that probably most congregations have a one-sided ministry. They attract one kind of people and serve them. But in every community is the possibility for using the same facility and resources to meet the needs of more than one kind of people. This is the possibility that we want to explore together now.

Among Singles

Jim Smoke, who was singles' director for the huge Crystal Cathedral and now works with Hollywood Presbyterian Church, says that work among singles today is the pioneering edge, similar to what work among teenage youth was 30 or 40 years ago.[1]

I heard him outline his program, with special activities for each ten-year age span. But what a staff that took. Only a large, rich church could ever embark on such a ministry, I thought.

Then I happened to read an article in a *Faith at Work* magazine entitled "Everybody Needs Family."[2] It told of a group that calls itself the "Black Sheep"—eight men and women who are members of the large, famous Marble Collegiate Church in New York City. But theirs is a small group. All are singles. They work at different kinds of jobs in different parts of the city. Each lives alone and has an extra need for the "family" they find together. They represent a cross section of middle-class professionals who share the Christian faith and the desire to make the most of their lives.

They didn't come together overnight. It took them a while to find each other and become a group. It began with a luncheon group that met for six weeks on Wall Street as part of their congregation's annual Lenten program.

They liked the luncheons but found the time limit frustrating. They had trouble finding a night when they could meet. Some dropped out, but three refused to give up.

As they talked, they discovered that in their own families each had been called "the black sheep," so that became their name. In one way or another, each of them had been a rebel—the first to leave home, or the one who went off and did something unexpected, or the one who left the small town for New York City.

The author of the article first went to Marble Collegiate Church almost in defiance, to show her mother she had not abandoned her faith. But something kept drawing her back. Eventually she found this set of friends.

The group doesn't follow any set pattern when they meet, but they spend a lot of time together. Often they eat an evening meal together. Sometimes they study the Bible; sometimes they share dreams and goals. Sometimes they just ventilate their frustrations of the day. They pray at the beginning and ending of everything they do—whether it is skiing together or cleaning the ivy beds around the church.

One member's father died of cancer, and the group came together to share in that grief. Another had a bout of her own cancer. "I'm scared to death," she said. "I don't know how to cope. I know I can't do it alone." Another had a special promotion at work, and they all celebrated.

As I read their story I thought, *That can even happen in a little church like one of mine!* A handful of singles who care about each other and have a dedication to the faith is all it takes. "Two or three in My name."

Indeed, the very smallness has strengths that a huge conglomerate of singles might miss entirely.

For the small group at Marble Collegiate, their group is not a dating resource. It *is* a resource for intimacy—not in the popular sense of sexual activity—but an intimacy of sharing and caring.

Most of our congregations could help foster such a ministry to a group in our midst.

Among the Deaf

A friend of mine, Bud Roufs, pastors the Salem Lutheran Church in Glendale, Calif. In his congregation was one deaf child and some parents who didn't want the silence barrier to shut their child off from full participation in the family of God. The mother began signing each service for her daughter. Other deaf persons began to come—four to six each Sunday.

The Glendale Club for the Deaf began to show their captioned films in the church's social hall on a weeknight. About 50 persons began to come. The church discovered that deaf people love occasions when the deaf are together. They love to stand and "chatter" without interference from a lot of hearing people.

Other activities developed, such as monthly luncheons.

The church began to provide an interpreter during worship, but the number in worship still remained about six to eight. But when the congregation had someone who would preach and sign together, the number of deaf people attending rose to near 20.

They discovered some reasons for this. The average reading ability of deaf people, even those with high school diplomas, is somewhere between the fifth and seventh grade.

When a person signs what another says, they also discovered, it is not simply English done with the hands. It has a completely different syntax and grammar.

Pastor Roufs asked the person who signs the service if it is like English. The person replied, "No, it is more like Chinese." Deaf people tend to think in symbols. Spoken sermons tend to be abstract and difficult for the deaf to relate to. They are forced into a strange, unfamiliar world.

The pastor discovered that many deaf people feel resentful toward the church because they have been excluded from meaningful participation all their lives.

In September 1980, the congregation secured a pastor for the deaf, John Soyster. At the installation, a Sunday evening service geared to the deaf, there was signed liturgical dance and there were mimes. Pastor Roufs described the evening as "truly exciting."

The deaf have been given their own place of worship, the church parlor, which is equipped with altar and pulpit. The entire service is signed. Everything is spoken and signed, or sung and signed, at the same time.

The average attendance grew to between 27 and 30 in five months. About half of those who attended were deaf. Others were friends, persons interested in learning to sign, or some simply curious people.

The experience is unique in the American Lutheran Church. While three other congregations in that communion have separate church buildings and organizations for the deaf, this is the first time a deaf congregation is a part of a hearing congregation.

This is the *homogeneous unit principle* (about which Church Growth experts theorize and critics love to argue) at its very best: reaching out to people in their own "heart language," permitting them entrance into the Kingdom of God in ways they can understand.

It is Salem's intent that the congregations should stay together. In this way, resources of place and program, of money and people, are readily available. Yet each group has its own identity and worships in its most meaningful ways.

Social Leper Colonies

In Jesus' day, people with leprosy were feared. With the disease, fingers, toes, hands, or feet might drop off. People avoided leprosy victims, not wanting to see distorted faces or a missing nose. The masses were terribly afraid that they, too, might contract the disease. Lepers were driven off to live in caves, to band together to try to scratch enough food to survive.

In our day, says George Hunter, there are *social leper colonies.*[4] He tells of a church that opened its doors for a party for *mentally handicapped children.* One night a month the children were brought to play together and be entertained.

While the children played, the parents stood and watched. Then someone from the church suggested that since their children were occupied, they might like to go to a nearby room and sit together and talk. There they began to share their struggles, their hopes, their fears, their uncertainties about the future, their problems, the burdens they bore.

Eighty families have become a part of that effort.

Another pastor of a very small church had a unique gift for *hospital visitation.* Sometimes the best of friends draw back from going to the hospital. Sick people are not the people many others most want to see. But this pastor did it well. As a result of his faithful, caring ministry, one after another of those he ministered to in a time of need and loneliness began to relate to that congregation.

The *elderly* are among those cut off many times. My wife is a night supervisor in a convalescent home. She has worked in many such homes and has seen the old deserted, all rights taken from them, forced into situations against their wills. Sometimes they are abused physically. A person with a mind that wanders but is still clear enough to know what is happening will cry out, "Don't hit me again; I'll do what you want." Some people are bruised, their bones are sometimes broken, limbs twisted. Some are abused by their own children.

Even in the church, the impact of the youth culture has told us that a senior high youth group or a young-couples' class is where the pay dirt is. A very small congregation will begin clamoring, "If only we had someone to develop a high school group. That's the future of the church."

The truth is that a very low percentage of any high school group stays on in that congregation to become the pillars.

Meanwhile, older people may be very near who are lonely and will eagerly respond to any attempt to reach out to them in love.

Other Cultures

Increasingly in many of our communities are people of other cultures. If they are to be reached, it must be by someone who speaks their languages and understands their needs, their dreams, their fears, their hopes.

One of the congregations I serve now has a Korean church and, more recently, a Spanish church. Each has services in its own language. With the Korean congregation we hold occasional shared services. We sing the same hymns—they in Korean and we in English. Their pastor and I alternate reading each verse of Scripture in one language and then the other. The sermon is preached a paragraph at a time and interpreted. We always share a noon meal of food from both cultures.

The beauty and integrity of each culture is preserved as we celebrate together our love for the Christ for whom red, yellow, black, and white are all precious.

The irrepressible Southern Baptists in the Los Angeles area each Sunday morning hold services in some 26 different languages. But even that is not enough, because 82 specific languages have been identified in the Los Angeles school district.

Any California school having ten or more children who speak a language must provide opportunity for them to continue to develop skills in their own language as well as in English. Can the church of Christ do less?

Congregational Church Planting

Dr. Carl Segerhammar, a leading Lutheran pastor in Southern California, served a 1,000-member congregation in downtown Los Angeles early in his ministry. During each of his nine years there, he took in an average of 100 new members.

Yet when he left that congregation, the membership was 150 less than on the day he began his ministry there. In the meantime, however, 18 new Lutheran congregations had been organized, and all but one of them started with a core of members from that mother congregation he served. Years later the congregation developed services within its own walls in Spanish, Finnish, and Korean.

That's a large church, you say. But your church and mine, however small, can be involved in the same kind of activity.

Across the country I know of many congregations which have a cluster of families in an area too far removed for regular, full participation. They can begin with a monthly evening Bible study and fellowship time for this group. They may grow to a church school and preaching service, maybe held in someone's family room. They may be serviced at first by the pastor of the mother church, who does double duty for a time.

One example: Larry Kemp pastors a 65-member Church of the Brethren congregation in Tucson, Arizona. He has discovered a cluster of 15 members who live 35 miles away in Avra Valley. Even in the wide-open spaces of Arizona, that is a long way to travel to church. Every Thursday the minister travels to Avra Valley to meet with them for fellowship and Bible study. They are ready now to begin services on a Sunday afternoon. A new church is being born.

Jack Redford, master church planter for the Southern Baptists, says, "One person with an open heart, an open Bible, and an open living room is sufficient to begin."[5]

And out of such fellowships, strong churches grow. Often both congregations are strengthened in giving and attendance as a result.

Universal Mandate

Some people resist everything about Church Growth because they feel a guilt trip has been laid on those who do not grow.

It needs to be said that *some faithful churches will not grow*. Indeed, some churches, because of special ministries or of a unique calling to a prophetic ministry, *should not expect* to make significant growth. There are congregations with a special witness that makes any measurable growth highly unlikely.[6]

But all congregations share in the mandate of the Great Commission. All of us, whatever our calling or unique ministry, must share in some way in the larger picture of God's passion that all might be drawn to Him.

This may mean being instrumental in church planting somewhere else. It may mean developing a ministry to other groups using our own facilities.

Rentals

At this point let me inject a note of caution: *"rentals" will not do it*. My own experience is that when an outside agency rents the church building for its program—a day-care group, a senior citizens program, or the Boy Scouts—the feed in to the church is almost nonexistent.

On the other hand, if the same kind of program can be provided as a ministry of the church, staffed at least in part by church people, the feed in to the church may be fairly high if the program is good.

A nursery school run by a secular organization at one of the churches I served brought in no one. But in another congregation where the nursery was still community-based but undergirded by excellent teachers from the church, the results were different. Family after family saw the beautifully equipped rooms for their children, thrilled to the excellent care and professional adequacy, and wanted that same quality of religious training at the church school hour.

Jack Redford puts it this way:

> We, as God's people, are to show God's love to all people. That's what community cultivation and church planting are all about: showing people that God loves them and that they need Jesus Christ in their lives. A word of caution: the love we show must be genuine; the care must come from the heart. The ministries begun—to senior citizens, Mother-Day-Out projects, day-care centers—demonstrate that a church loves people, is concerned about people, and is in the community to help meet the real needs of people. If we want to build churches anywhere in the world, we must build bridges to people. We reach people by becoming friends with them, by meeting a need, or by becoming involved in an area of interest.[7]

So the rule of thumb is: *minimize rentals*. Begin at the point of need in your community, and provide that service yourself out of your own love.

Opportunity Around Us

To state Robert Schuller's secret of success again: "Find a need and meet it. Find a hurt and heal it."

There are hurting people all around us, rejected or bypassed by society—blind, deaf, handicapped, retarded, elderly, and even singles, who are making up an increasingly larger portion of our society.

The place to start may be within your own congregation. Is there a handicapped person, a blind or deaf person, someone with a retarded child? Do they have friends who would respond to a ministry that your congregation, however small, might begin to develop?

Do we have the eyes to see those who are hurting? They are there. Do we have the ears to hear their cries, the minds to discern their special needs? Do we have the hands and hearts and the wills to reach out and bring them in?

Teaching Helps for Chapter 8

Before the class session:

☐ Prepare your own list of "social leper colonies" in your community. Check with some people who work at social service vocations or with pastors. Let the participants suggest their ideas first. Be ready to add to their list.

☐ Prepare the "Many-sided ministry" transparency.

☐ Prepare a copy of Medical Chart 9 for each student.

Suggested Lesson Plan

1. Look together at Medical Chart 9. Opposite the arrow pointing to the upper right, list the kind of church you are, the values you have, whom you minister to. Then, going clockwise, list some of the groups of your area that are not ministered to. You do not need to place a name opposite every arrow, only those where a group can genuinely be designated.

At the bottom, note the question. Maybe there is a deaf person in your congregation or in one of the families related to your congregation. Maybe there is someone physically handicapped who goes to a school for the handicapped and might have circles of contact. Are there places where your church might logically begin a ministry? Pick one, if one seems evident.

2. What are the social leper colonies in your community? Can you list some?

Think of a person or group that is ministering in some way to a "social leper." Invite that person to share joys, frustrations, and expectations. Explore together whether that ministry could be enlarged and become a part of the church's ministry.

3. No matter what your size, do not overlook the possibility of establishing an outpost Bible study or church school, which might develop into another congregation. The Nigerian Church of the Brethren is one of the fastest growing in the world! One of the requirements for any fellowship that seeks to be accepted as a full congregation is that it first must have established another new fellowship. A cluster of a few families in a geographically distant community is enough. Is it possible for you?

4. Discuss the paragraph: ''Some faithful churches will not grow. Indeed, some churches, because of special ministries or because of unique calling to a prophetic ministry, should not expect to make significant growth.'' Can you think of any examples?

Go on to discuss the next paragraph: ''But all congregations share in the mandate of the Great Commission.''

5. Look at the statement ''Rentals will not do it.'' Do you have rentals performing services that your church might assume as a ministry?

6. Let individuals review experiences with their prospects. Also, review progress in the congregation.

7. Read together Mark 6:30-34. Reflect on the kind of ministry Christ wants us to have.

1. Jim Smoke in a presentation to a ministerial fellowship at Glendale, Calif.

2. Joan Sonntag, ''Everybody Needs Family,'' *Faith at Work* (Volume XCII, Number 2, March 1979), pp. 7-9.

3. The Assemblies of God, Lutheran Church Missouri Synod, and Southern Baptists are leading the way in forming deaf congregations.

4. At Institute for American Church Growth Advanced Growth Seminar, January 1981, Pasadena, Calif.

5. One of the best outlines of procedures to use in establishing a new congregation is Jack Redford's *Planting New Churches* (Nashville: Broadman Press, 1978). It has a Southern Baptist flavor, but its basics are applicable to any denomination. Quote is from p. 62.

6. Examples might be the Church of the Savior in Washington, D.C., which has made membership standards so high only a few will join. In the deep South during times of racial tension and in South Africa today, some congregations have provided a bold witness to the Gospel of Christ by worshiping as an integrated community of faith. The Confessing Church of Germany, which spoke unashamedly against the evils of Nazi rule, is such an example. Churches in sparsely populated communities may be an example, but often they, too, have non-Christian neighbors living in their midst. There *are* exceptions. But they are *few*.

7. Jack Redford, *Planting . . .*, p. 20.

Medical Chart 9

List some of the groups around us to which we could minister. Are there singles, handicapped, deaf, some other cultural group?

Are there groups to which we already have entrance?

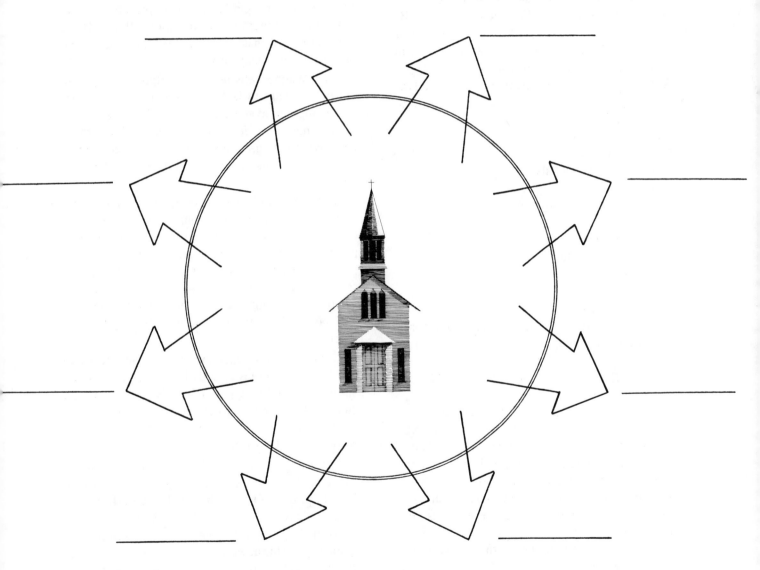

9 To Everyone a Gift

One of the keys to a growing congregation is to discover and utilize its gifts of the Spirit. In the New Testament gifts or energies were given to every member of Christ's body.

New Testament Background

A number of passages talk of gifts of the Spirit: Romans 12:6-8; I Corinthians 12:4-11; Ephesians 4:11-16; I Peter 4:9-11. Ephesians 4:12 (GNB) suggests that the gifts are given "to prepare all of God's people for the work of Christian service, in order to build up the body of Christ."

As we list the gifts, we sense that they cover all the elements needed for the care, growth, and strengthening of a congregation:

preaching—inspiration
teaching—nurture
witnessing—evangelists
encouragement
serving—hospitality—caring
stewardship
leadership—administration
wisdom—knowledge
miracles—faith
prophetic witness
worship—tongues—interpretation

We are all gifted toward various divisions of labor in order to be a functioning part of the Body of Christ.

Four Truths About Spiritual Gifts

Four points are suggested by the Scriptures.
I Peter 4:7-11 tells us much. Verse 10 (GNB) says, "Each one, as a good manager of God's different gifts, must use for the good of others the special gift he has received from God."

The first point that is important for us is that *every Christian has been given gifts*. Each of us has gifts that are uniquely his.

I read an amazing interview with Pete Rose, the proud, aggressive baseball player.[1] "I can't run fast," he said. "I never could throw too well. But I can hit. And I've only missed nine games in ten years and none since I came to the Phillies."

So it is with the gifts of the Spirit.

Everyone has gifts, given by God Himself. And each of us is charged with a holy charge to discover what gifts God has given.

The second point that comes through all of the passages on gifts is that *our gifts differ*.

The apostle Paul compares the church to the parts of a body.[2] We are not all a hand. We are not all a foot, or a mouth. One person may preach. Another may be a teacher. Some have the gift of hospitality—of making others feel comfortable and at home. Some may serve.

Peter Wagner tells how he went as a young man out of seminary to Bolivia, thinking he would become a great evangelist—"the Billy Graham of South America." He spent hours on his first sermon and gave it with great flourish. He practiced in front of a mirror so that he even held the Bible like Billy Graham.

At the end of his masterpiece, he gave the invitation and expected to see throngs of Bolivians come down the aisle. But as people sang the closing song, not one person moved to accept Christ.

He was shattered. What was wrong? He went to some of the other missionaries. They asked him whether his sermon was Scripturally based. Maybe it had too much of himself and not enough of God's Word.

So Wagner went back to pore over Scripture and build a much more Biblically laden message. Again he spent long hours practicing. He gave what he thought was another masterpiece. Again he gave the invitation at the close . . . and waited . . . and again no one came forward.

Again he went to his missionary friends, and as they talked with him they raised the question, had he been in prayer? Or was this his human effort?

So again he went back and spent even more time. This time he gave many hours to fervent prayer. And again he gave his newest masterpiece and offered the invitation, and again . . . no one came forward. Not one.

Finally it began to dawn on him that maybe his gifts did not include being an evangelist. Gradually

Peter Wagner came to realize that one of his gifts was teaching. When he taught, people learned. Today he is a great teacher.

There is an old, old story about the man who saw writing in the sky—the letters "P.C."—clear as can be, and assumed he had been called to "preach Christ." After a few sermons, some kind friends informed him they thought what those letters probably were calling him to do was to "plant corn." Or maybe "park cars."

Our gifts differ. They are not the same.

The third point in all the verses about gifts is that *each of the gifts is important*–including yours.

When Albert Einstein was invited to join the staff of the Institute for Advanced Study at Princeton, he was asked what yearly payment would be acceptable. He told the directors he would leave that up to them. When they objected to this, he suggested that they talk with his wife.

"Let her decide," he said. "Then she won't be able to complain that I don't give her enough money to run the house."

So it was arranged. He never did bother to ask what figure was agreed on.[3]

As talents in the secular world differ, as even a genius like Einstein may be a child when it comes to handling money, so with the gifts God gives us.

Our gifts and talents differ, but *each* is important.

One member may enrich my life with *music*. Another may *prick my conscience* with some issue that I as a Christian must be concerned about. Another may have the ability to *listen* when I am hurting. Another may bring *cheer* when there is discouragement. One may *teach*. Another may open his home with *graciousness*. Another has the gift of *humor*.

All the gifts and resources God gives are important.

The fourth point is that the gifts God has given us are to be *used for the good of all*. Each one of us, as a good manager of God's different gifts, must use *for the good of others* the special gift he has received from God.

None of us dare take our gift, wrap it in a napkin, and bury it in the ground. We are all robbed when someone in our midst does not share his gift.

But even more important, to fail to share is to withhold what God has entrusted to you. And to withhold is to have to answer to God Himself one day. He expects you to use what He has given. From everyone to whom much is given, much shall be required.

Spiritual Gifts and Talents: Not the Same

God gives *spiritual* gifts to every Christian. We may use our *talents* to fulfill these gifts.

The friend who typed this manuscript said it was not until three years ago that she named her spiritual gift. As a result of a gifts seminar in her congregation, she and her husband discovered that they both have been given the spiritual gift of teaching. She fulfills this gift through the talent of writing. Her husband fulfills the same gift through art.

We can discover our gifts by observing how we respond to specific situations. Imagine a church social, where a spastic knocks over a cup of coffee and spills a plate of food onto the floor. The person with the gift of *service* may be the first to kneel down and clean up the mess.

One with the gift of *mercy* may immediately throw an arm around the person and show loving support.

Another may respond by saying, "If only we were better *organized*, this would never have happened."

And still another might suggest, "We need classes to *train* us for just such occasions."

We respond differently. And how we respond tells much about the gift of the Spirit that is ours.

Each gift has characteristics. Alice and Roger Schrage, who lead gifts seminars, have provided some of the most helpful thinking for me.[4]

They suggest that why you do what you do is a more important key to discovering your gift than what you do. They ask, "What is the payoff for you? Some things we do are hard going. Others bring joy. What brings the joy for you?"

Alice comments that, in their seminars, she loves

working one-on-one where possible. The joy for her is in encouraging others *(exhortation),* listening to people, responding to their needs.

Her husband, Roger, comes to the seminars with the gift of organization or *administration.* He wants churches to stop spinning their wheels, stop trying to put square pegs into round holes, become more efficient vehicles for God.

Both share in the same task but from very different motivations. Their approach includes taking Biblical materials and looking at qualities found there.

For example, *prophecy.* They approach prophecy by looking at people like Isaiah and Jeremiah. What were the qualities in their lives? And what are the qualities in the lives of Christians with similar gifts today? Prophets cared very much about speaking God's truth, about speaking even if it meant being alone and rejected. People with the prophetic witness today are very much the same.

Alice and Roger have grouped the spiritual gifts found in Romans 12 in an attempt to help people discover their own gifts. They use three categories—*supportive* gifts, *verbal* gifts, and *operational* gifts. Within these, each of us may be able to find ourselves.

SUPPORTIVE gifts include:

A. *The gift of exhortation.* (The Good News Bible says "to encourage others.") This person responds to life-related spiritual problems.

Qualities the Schrages list include the following:

Practical–analyzes problems and wants steps taken to deal with them.

Sensitive to emotional/spiritual needs and to potential others may not see in people.

Listens to what people say about their problems; sometimes senses the unspoken messages also.

Interacts–works with the person in need.

B. *The gift of service.* This person responds to practical human needs. Qualities include:

Practical–wants to take care of needs.

Sensitive to needs and to insensitivity in others.

Active–tends to rush in with help, sometimes not listening or hearing what is being said because of busyness. (Alice observes that often people with the gift of service don't feel they have any gifts. Meanwhile they are busy serving "like crazy.")

C. *The gift of mercy.* This person responds to how people *feel.*

Emotional–may simply listen and sympathize, doing other things only to show identification with feelings.

Sensitive to insensitivity of others; senses how individuals feel and the mood of the group.

Listens–greatest strength is in empathy and forgiveness.

(Alice comments that mercy people are less action-oriented. Most mercy people don't go anywhere; others come to them, and they just listen. The best example she knows, she says, is a woman instrumental in settling two Vietnamese families. Much of her time is spent simply sitting with them, listening to them.)

A second grouping of gifts of the Spirit goes under the heading of *VERBAL* gifts. These include:

A. *The gift of prophecy.* The prophet is concerned about exposing sin and wrong.

Speaks, often eloquently, against sin.

Studies to know what God has to say about sin.

Authoritarian because of concern about sin. The prophet may appear to lack sensitivity about people's feelings and the practical circumstances.

B. *The gift of teaching.* The teacher is concerned about validating true doctrine.

Speaks to give proper, complete background for doctrine.

Studies to verify the validity of the church's teachings; sometimes prefers the study to the presenting of facts.

Authoritarian–may appear insensitive and overly concerned about details of study.

The third area is *OPERATIONAL* gifts:

A. *The gift of giving.* This person responds generously to financial needs.

Awareness of resources–knows how to make and use money.

Sense of participation–gives to those people or programs that minister directly, and feels very much a part of the ministry.

Manner–gives quietly so others often are not aware of it.

B. *The gift of administration* (organization). This person responds to need by managing resources to accomplish goals.

Aware of resources–knows the limitations of both people and money.

Involvement–delegates task, not becoming involved in details; may allow details to go unattended at times.

Manner–waits to be called upon by those in charge, but often assumes leadership where none exists.

As you survey the people you know best, can you find some fitting one of these categories? As I read these I thought, "That's Ken!" "That fits Paul." "That's Nora." "That sure describes Jean!" What about yourself? Does one category describe you, your feelings, the area where you find joy?

The secret is first to find your own gift, and then to discover your own unique talents and begin to blend them into a beautiful symphony of loving, joyous service.

Roger comments that in real life we all face tasks that may be outside the area of our gifts. There are jobs for us all that "go with the territory," things that simply need to be done.

But how freeing it is to know our own gifts, to know the areas where we move easily and with confidence and joy, and then to begin to build in those areas rather than struggling to do what is not within our area of strength and ability.

Discovering and Using Our Gifts

As Peter Wagner explores the use of spiritual gifts in his comprehensive book on the subject, he lists five steps toward discovering and deploying your particular gifts.[5]

1. *Explore the possibilities*. Define the gifts, talk about them, study the Biblical passages. "If you're eighteen and haven't discovered your spiritual gifts," he comments, "don't worry. It may be too early yet. If you are twenty-five and haven't discov-

ered them . . . worry." It takes a while, often four to twelve months for new Christians.

2. *Experiment* with as many as you can. Ask yourself, "Do I have this gift?" But also, more important, ask yourself, "Do I *not* have this gift?"

3. *Examine your feelings*. God gives us resources we enjoy using. I know a wonderful baritone soloist. When he sings, people are moved. When I have asked him to read Scripture, his knees have turned to jelly.

4. *Evaluate your effectiveness*. Almost every spiritual gift is task-oriented. If your effort at a certain gift doesn't do the job, your gift may lie someplace else.

5. *Expect confirmation from the Body*. Others will help you find your gift.

I would have to add that, for me, an understandings of gifts has come in my fortieth year as a Christian that I had no idea were present in my thirtieth year. God can and does move us in new directions as we live life for Him.

Pastor Bud Roufs's exciting experiment in developing a ministry to the deaf grew out of a real need in their midst. One day at a pastor's luncheon he said to me, "I think that's what I Corinthians 12 means when it talks about gifts. We discover our gifts as we sense a need that we discover we are able to fill and we fill it with excitement and joy. The best ministries of the church," he continued, "do not come as the pastor or the board thinks up things to do. The best ministries grow out of our own life and experience."

You are not asked to do everything. You are asked to do—expected to do—the things you are uniquely fitted to do.

The most beautiful example I know of this is a woman in the first church I served in Harrisburg, Pa. She and her husband were middle-aged with no children, although she loved children. She was in the adult choir. Her brother was in charge of the choirs in a large suburban Pittsburgh high school and directed choir festivals all over Pennsylvania.

She had taught church school. It had not been a good experience for her, and she refused that job at each new invitation. She had been asked to serve on committees, but she knew that, too, was not an area where she felt at home. She was quiet. She felt she did not contribute much.

Finally it occurred to me that she loved children and she loved music. We were wanting to start a children's choir. Why not Norma?

She said, "Yes." Immediately! With enthusiasm!

And she *loved* it. It was a situation where her unique gifts and talents perfectly matched a need.

That is what must begin to happen for each of us. Some cannot sing in the choir. Some are not able to teach. Some are not good at reading or praying in public. Some are not helpful at painting or carpentry or sewing. Some make terrible visitors. Some hate serving on boards and committees with a passion.

But every one of us has gifts and talents that God has given us. And they are different from the gifts and talents of others. They are to be uncovered and used for the good of all, or we will not complete the task of becoming what God wants of us.

And as every Christian is helped to discover his or her gifts and then develops the talents to use them, the church is strengthened, and the church grows.

Grow the Skeleton

John Wimber left his job as a Church Growth consultant a few years ago and started a church in Yorba Linda, Calif. It still meets in a rented auditorium but has several thousand members. One of the keys, he says, is *"If you grow the skeleton, the body will take care of itself."*

Every person recruited for a job in the church results, on the average (says John Wimber), in *2.8 other people* who will automatically come. As people discover their gifts and become involved in the church—ushering or teaching or choir or whatever—we get a dividend of 2.8 relatives and/or friends. If you have 10 people involved in your choir and 20 involved as leaders and helpers in your church school and worship, the likelihood is you will have at least 84 others in attendance related to those 30.

As soon as we had a handful of men who were not already involved in the choir, we organized usher teams that serve for one month three times a year. There is a head usher who oversees. Each team has a captain. But when those men, some of them not all that active, are on usher duty, they are present with their families. Gradually they become woven into the life of the church.

Keep tab on the skeleton, grow the skeleton, and the body will take care of itself.

We have not because we *plan* not. Most churches keep church school records and membership records, but they don't *use* them. If a grocery store knows how many cans of peas it has, it is not just for the sake of knowing. We need to go over the records until every person finds involvement at the point of gifts.

An excellent exercise is to have people on the board and in every group in the church *list as many meaningful tasks* as they can related to their area of interest. Those who counsel parents of teenagers know that youth resist busywork. But work related to the family's survival and well-being is often tackled with regularity and commitment. It is that way for adults. Discover as many important areas of work as you can—from caring for a flower bed, to being secretary for a group to developing the library, to becoming a co-teacher in a church school class. How many additional people can you put to meaningful work?

Michelangelo went to the marble quarry one winter day believing that if he could find the right block of stone, he could create a masterpiece.

The other artists had been there before him. Only one jagged, irregular piece of marble was left. The others had passed it by, seeing no possible art in it.

Michelangelo studied it, then accepted it and ordered the discarded stone taken to his shop. He worked on it for months, and from that misshapen fragment he produced his magnificent statue "David."

Later he said, "Its outline was dictated by the imperfections of the block I worked with. The bend of the head, the twist of the body, the arm holding the sling. They were all there in that jagged, irregular piece of rock."

God sees the imperfect, jagged chunk that is each of us. But the great Artist-Craftsman also sees the possibilities for beauty in each of us.

Frank Lloyd Wright, the great American architect, was the son and grandson of preachers. Speaking to students one time he said, "A stream can rise no higher than its source. You cannot give more to architecture than you are. So go to work upon yourselves, to make yourselves, in quality, what you would have your buildings be."[6]

All God would do in our world must start with you and me. He has given us spiritual gifts and endowed us with many talents, all the resources we need to accomplish His exciting will where we are. Our task is to uncover those rich resources and to dedicate them—to put them to work.

I once heard a denominational leader, Truman Douglas, tell New York City congregations they ought to wipe the slate clean of appointments to their boards and committees and start all over. He suggested using a large chalkboard and on one side listing the needs around them and within their group. On the other side they were to list the talents and the gifts that were present in the group.

Our organization should not take the shape of long-standing committees that may have served well in the past, but are of less-than-adequate value today. Our organization should take shape around needs and around the resources God has given to our fellowship.

As we involve people, as we help them discover who in God's name they are and what He intends for them to be become, the church cannot help but grow. Naturally.

Teaching Helps for Chapter 9

Before the class session:

☐ Again, the seating will need to be movable.

☐ Ask a committee of church chairpersons to list as many meaningful jobs related to their areas as they can that could use volunteers.

☐ Prepare copies of Medical Chart 10 for each student.

☐ Prepare copies of the groups of gifts.

Suggested Lesson Plan

1. Look together at the three groupings of gifts. Guide the members in first trying to locate yourselves. Does one of them describe the kind of Christian you are? Place your own initials after the one that is "you." Then suggest where some others in your congregation are, as you know them. Indicate their placement with their initials.

    I. *SUPPORTIVE GIFTS*
        A. Encouragement
        B. Service
        C. Mercy
    II. *VERBAL GIFTS*
        A. Prophetic witness
        B. Teaching
    III. *OPERATIONAL GIFTS*
        A. Giving
        B. Administration

Share your findings with each other.

2. Distribute copies of Medical Chart 10 and follow the instructions at the bottom. Elaborate a bit regarding the final column: "*Why* do you enjoy this certain activity? What is the payoff for you? Is it because (a) you *care about people,* or because you are seeking to (b) *share a message,* or because you (c) like *organizing?* Which?"

If your group is large, divide into smaller groups of six to eight. Let each person share his talents. Let each of the others in the group tell the person sharing what strengths they see in him. Help each other discover gifts.

Take time to affirm gifts as a group. "I see Mary's gifts as _____ , _____ , and _____ . Let's affirm that for her by saying, 'Mary, your gifts are to _____ , _____ , and _____ .' These gifts are yours to build up the Body of Christ. As you use these gifts, the church (our group) will be stronger and the Kingdom of God will be richer. The group will affirm this with you by saying, 'Amen.' "

3. Together list as many meaningful jobs in your congregation as you can think of. Ask every board, committee, and group in the church to add to the list.

Assign someone or some committee to involve as many people as possible at the point of their gift or talent. In other words, build the "skeleton."

4. Update each other on the progress with your personal prospects and with the status of congregational growth.

5. Read together Matthew 25:14-30. Covenant together to help each other in discovering and using gifts and talents.

6. Have each person pray silently for every person present, silently naming them and lifting them into the presence of God, seeking to discover the treasures God has placed within them to be used "for the glory of God and our neighbor's good."

1. *Los Angeles Times,* September 9, 1980, sec. IV, p. 2.
2. Romans 12:4, 5; I Corinthians 10:17; 12:12; Colossians 3:15.
3. *Quote* magazine, August 11, 1980, p. 163.
4. Discover Your Gifts Seminar, 1456 N. Wilson, Pasadena, CA 91104.
5. C. Peter Wagner, *Your Spiritual Gifts Can Help Your Church Grow* (Glendale, Calif.: Regal, 1979), p. 116ff.
6. Frank S. Mead, *Tarbell's Teacher's Guide, September 1979-August 1980* (Old Tappan, N.J.: Revell, 1979), p. 370.

Medical Chart 10

1. Indicate with an X how you feel about each item listed.
2. Underline the 3 to 5 you enjoy most. Which are most satisfying to you?
3. Fill in the final column for these.
4. Circle those that others tell you you are especially good at.
5. Share the results. Check them out with the group.

	Enjoy	Resist	Why do you enjoy? What gift applies?
Visiting in homes of members			
Singing			
Working with my hands at repair			
Cooking, preparing meals			
Teaching adults			
Working with teenagers			
Serving on committees			
Talking to others about my faith			
Being with young children			
Hospital visitation			
Listening to others share their problems			
Staying out of sight but working hard			
Organizing events			
Ushering, greeting visitors			
Keeping records			
Being with people in times of distress			
Giving all I can financially			
Entertaining guests in my home			
Exploring hard social problems			
Working for peace, justice			
Joining in prayer circle			
Creative writing			
Caring for babies			
Leading in worship			
Service to the down-and-out			
Working with finances			
Responding to those seeking spiritual counsel			
Helping establish a new congregation			
Responding to emergencies			
Drama			
Mowing lawn			
Art			
Counting offerings			
Painting walls			

10 The Power and the Glory

I saw a carefully lettered saying from Teilhard de Chardin framed and hanging in the outer office of a psychologist friend. "Joy," it said, "is the most infallible sign of the presence of God."

Some pastors, as they look out over the congregation, are convinced that the people have all been baptized in vinegar.

But joy is a fruit of the Spirit (Gal. 5:22)—one of the products of God's presence. Where God is, there is joy! And people cannot be blamed for not wanting to be part of a Godless, joyless group.

If God is not there, and joy is not there, our most heroic efforts will be in vain.

Sir Thomas Beecham once described the frustrations of being a guest conductor. Because he and the musicians were strangers to each other and rehearsal time was limited, the resulting performances were rarely artistic triumphs.

Once, after conducting a concert in a European capital, Beecham returned to London.

"How did it go?" a friend asked.

Sir Thomas made a face.

"What did they play?"

"I don't know what they played," shrugged Beecham. "I conducted Mozart."

How often has God been conducting "Mozart" and we, His people, have been playing our own thing? It may have sounded good to us, but it resulted in chaos and disruption and hurt lives.

It's God's Church

One of our members in a time of frustration several years into my pastoral leadership said, "Maybe we should just sell the church and let those of us who are left meet together on occasion in our homes."

My response shot back: "Then you would be a club, but not a church."

It is *God's* church that we are building. And the glory is not to us but to Him.

How important it is to get that straight.

When it is His, all kinds of things get done.

It has been said that you can accomplish almost anything if you don't care who gets the credit.

I like an old Chinese poem that hangs in my brother-in-law's kitchen. He grew up in a missionary home in China and is now preparing to return to China to work in village health. The poem reads:

> Go to the people.
> Live among them.
> Learn from them.
> Love them.
> Start with what they know.
> Build on what they have.
>   But of their best leaders
>   When their task is accomplished,
>   Their work is done,
>   The people all remark,
>   "We have done it ourselves."

When we can get ourselves out of the way, we open many doors. And with God all things are possible.

If the church is God's and if He gets the glory, there is no limit to what can happen. He has power to accomplish any task He places in our hands.

And if the glory is to God and not to us, then the bottom line is not the great choir we develop, or the moving worship service, or the captivating program.

Those things may speak more of glory to us than to God.

Reaching People Is the Main Thing

McGavran wrote in his book, *Understanding Church Growth*, about "redemption and lift."[1]

On the mission field a station is established. Sick people are given treatment. They learn what good medical care is all about. Some enter the mission school. They become educated. They learn how to farm, how to fertilize their ground for better production. They grow larger chickens and produce larger eggs. They learn about nutrition and about sanitary ways of living.

As these people from a very primitive, poverty-stricken society become Christians and learn the ways of the missionary, they become separated from the very people from whom they came. Never again can they live as they lived before. And in a short time, they actually come to look down upon the old life. They want no part of it again.

"Redemption and lift." Wherever the Gospel of Christ has gone, people have been lifted—given not only a new orientation of the soul but a whole new way of living that sets them apart and separates them from their own people.

Two generations ago, the people who had lived in the neighborhood of the church I served in Harrisburg, Pa., were attracted by a little old lady who organized a church school. The pastor with his booming voice and the sounds of gospel songs caught their attention. As they came, they began to see life differently. They put aside wasteful habits that drained all their resources. Getting blind drunk was no longer a pattern of life. They wanted education for their children and sent them off to Elizabethtown College, the denominational school.

As their children came back from college, they bought new homes in the suburbs. The language of the street was no longer theirs. The values of the street were no longer theirs. And they did not want their children even exposed to what they themselves had lived among but a few short years before.

Redemption and lift.

Lift is important. That is what Jesus came to do: to seek and to save (Lk. 19:10). To reach out and take hold and lift us all to something better.

But as we are lifted, we may come to confuse cultural tastes with the Gospel itself. We may come to let what has grown slowly in us become a barrier to others who would travel the same route but cannot because we have put too much distance between them and ourselves. We begin to say we want *quality*. But we usually reveal a kind of snobbishness.

In every church I've served, the temptation is to give people what we think they "need" (which may be more a cultural preference) than to start where people are. We look down our noses at the simpler tunes with which many people identify. Jack Redford tells how as an army chaplain he was very successful with officers. But his next assignment was with recruits, and he was a flop. He decided to

get an evangelist to preach for him, who introduced gospel songs he hated. But the chapel filled up.

The question is not whether we offer a cheap theology or water down basic convictions. The question is whether we are willing to *start where people are* and let them grow as we have grown.

"Would you do it?" McGavran asks.[2] "Would you cease importing culturally foreign music and worship into settings where these forms are not natural?" Would you, if you could, reach hundreds now shut out?

Among a group of people who think Bach is a beer and Haydn is a quarterback with the Los Angeles Rams, are we willing to approach people in their own "heart language"?

Our forefathers did this. In seminary, those in the field of music argued for "the finest music" to be sung in church. But Luther took his tunes from the taverns of the day.

The United Methodist Church brought blessing to millions around the world, partly because it let people come to Christ in ways that were natural to them, ways that were a long step removed from the stately worship of the Anglican churches of 1750.

The Wesleys paid a price for putting faith in the forms of the street people. Translators who dared render the Bible in the vernacular of the people were burned at the stake, or ridiculed and derided while their Bibles were destroyed.

In Wesley's day, the people would not go into the cathedrals, but they would come to open meetings. John Wesley believed outdoor meetings were an obscenity. But he swallowed his feelings to engage the masses on their own turf.

Charles Wesley was a High Church musician. He loved Gregorian chants. But he recognized that the working people did not resonate to that but loved the music of the pubs. So he began writing hymns to the music of the pubs. He believed that reaching people was more important than his own aesthetic preferences.

How important is it that the people be reached? And if the things that bring their minds to God are first of all some simple hymn tune they have seen in a

Western movie as a child, or the mood they recall from childhood experiences in church with parents, that may be where we need to *start,* at least, if we genuinely want to reach them.

Can you sift through the chaff and discern what for you is basic and hold fast to that? Never let go of what is basic. But begin to translate that into other people's languages. Put it in terms they can understand, in styles to which they can easily relate.

Learning to Share Our Faith

In workshops I have conducted coast to coast, people say, "We need help in learning how to share our faith. When a neighbor or friend asks us about what Christ means to us, we don't know where to begin."

I suspect that not only many lay people feel this way, but many pastors as well.

I recall in my first pastorate we were selling "Broadway Bonds" to finance the building of a big new Christian education addition. We sold them to members, to friends, to family. But then I ran out of close friends. For the first time in my life I found myself talking to the man who owned the service station at the foot of the hill just down from my home. I found myself talking to my barber, to the people I knew at the checkout counter of the supermarket where I shopped, to the man who always sold me my suits. Not about Christ yet, but about my church and its need to build and the challenge it faced.

How difficult it is for some of us to talk to others about the things that are most meaningful to us. Perhaps we draw back because we feel that some have made what is so precious and sacred seem almost cheap by high-pressure tactics. Others of us by nature take the soft-sell approach in anything. We are as repulsed by vacuum sweeper salesmen and department store clerks who come on too strong as we are by those who hammer religion at strangers.

But the other day as I had breakfast with my encyclopedia salesman friend, an executive in his company, I noticed he stopped on the way to our cars to talk to a woman with some children getting into her car. He gave her his calling card, with a full-color picture of his books on one side and his name and phone number on the other. It was as natural as saying, "Good morning," with him. He commented to me, "You never know who may be interested."

Can each of us find ways to share a priceless treasure that are in keeping with our manner, our personality, with what seems to us to have integrity?

Tom Hanks raised the question in *Eternity* magazine some years ago about why the Holy Spirit is so undiscerning as to bless "cheap patterns of evangelism." Why is it that God does not bless our superior packaging of the Gospel?

As a harsh critic, Hanks joined Campus Crusade for Christ for a short time to try to find out what was happening. There he saw frightened youths come together and then go out to witness. He commented with amazement about the "poise that came to them." Campus Crusade insisted they *point* as they witnessed. This was difficult for them. But as they did it, they grew in strength and confidence. A joy and radiance came to their lives.

Hanks wrote: "The Holy Spirit, in a seemingly undiscerning way, was blessing their efforts in an unprecedented manner."

Then he read Luke 10 and discovered what seemed to be the training manual of the early church: what to do, what not to do, how to respond when offered unkosher food.

Hanks's conclusion was "If you are going to reach large numbers, *you need to put the cookies on the lower shelf.*"

Again, let us say it as clearly as possible: the plea is never to compromise basic convictions or faith but rather to translate faith into terms and ways that people can understand.

Surely one of the best results of the Mormon door-to-door missionary effort is not the number of converts. As we have indicated, that is low indeed. The most powerful result may be *what happens in the lives of those youth* as they share, meet hostility day after day, witness and witness again, face volleys of hard questions, seek to find the right word, the right answer, the winning key to heart after heart. They

"Don't ever play hide-and-go-seek with Mr. Wilson...he don't *SEEK*."

Dennis the Menace® cartoon courtesy of Hank Ketcham and © by Field Enterprises, Inc.

will never be the same again. The rest of their lives they will know a faith so thoroughly that virtually nothing will be able to dislodge it.

Learning from Salespeople

Encyclopedia salespeople know that their best chances for sales are with people who already have personal ties into their product. They know about that Church Growth principle. But they continue to reach out through ads, chance meetings, and blind door-to-door calling, too. No stone is left unturned for the purpose of selling books with some educational value.

We can learn from them.

These salespeople learn that "prospecting" is a continual process.[3] If you would succeed, they say, "you must develop a constant awareness *to prospecting with all your daily contacts.*" (How about that for a single-minded purpose?) "*Every activity in which you take part* provides you with an opportunity for more prospecting."

Contrast that with most of us, who divide life into little segments. We think religion from 10 to 12 on Sunday morning only.

Some methods of prospecting are:

Radiation: securing names and pertinent information about neighbors, friends, relatives, associates, others from *every* interview with *every* prospect. (One pastor of a growing congregation said, "After the death of a 14-year-old in the neighborhood, I worked with every friend he had.")

Centers of influence: ask influential "third parties" to name prospects.

Newspaper prospecting: watch for births, PTA activities, Scouting, school, and 4-H news. Look for honor roll, social, business, and community information.

Nest prospecting: work with people who have a common bond within one "unit," such as office, plant, business, industry, institution, school, grade, PTA group, bridge club, women's or Scouting group. (There are "networks" of people, McGavran has said. Use them.)

Observational prospecting: look for signs of children—Halloween or Christmas decorations, play or gym equipment in the yard, bicycles in the driveway, basketball nets. Make a note for future calling.

Cold canvassing: inquire at the first house on the street or the house that seems *least likely* to contain a prospect. Ask, "If you were calling on these people, whom would you call on first?" "What is the best time to find them home?" *Qualifying* your leads will help assure you of genuine prospects and greatly help your planning.

At the end of each day in the field, transfer your leads to file cards and keep your prospect file up-to-date. Keep an ongoing record of visits to avoid duplication. Use a notebook to list each street or route by block and house number. When a call is made, record the date and use a simple code to show the result of that call.

Church Growth theory talks about going to receptive people. Salespeople learn to distinguish between prospects who are likely to be interested and those who are not. "Make the decision as early as possible to avoid wasting your valuable time."

The estimate is that about 10 percent of us have the gift of evangelism. Only about one in ten has the gift of leading numbers of people step by step into a living relationship with Christ. But in a similar way few of us have the gift of "stewardship," at least in the sense of giving as much as 90 percent of our income to Christ's work. Yet all of us are called to be stewards as a part of our discipleship. And all of us are called to share our faith as part of our discipleship.

Every congregation can help its people grow in this. Church school lessons can include more discussion questions that help people articulate their faith in small, safe, discussion groups. Sometimes asking a person to be prepared to share in a specific area helps.

Sometimes sharing times in the worship may be used to ask someone to talk for five minutes about how his or her faith has affected work or life decisions or views on a certain area.

We can help to set the tone, too, in our classes and in our worship by avoiding the use of well-worn phrases that mean much to us but absolutely nothing to those outside. Sometimes we are as bad as a bunch of doctors or lawyers in the way we allow our language to be so totally separated from life. Can we help each other state our faith in noncliche terms? Can we put terms like *grace* and *saved* and even *precious* in language others will receive with freshness and understanding?

Next Door

The best place to start is not far away.

A pastor friend, Chuck Thompson, serving the nearby Community Church of God (Anderson) in Glendale, led a campaign to build up the church school. They visited door to door in their community. They used colorful brochures. They handed out bumper stickers and colorful posters. They gave prizes one week to the person who brought the most people, another week to the class with the highest percentage of increase. After five weeks of intensive effort, their church school went from about 40 members to more than 100; it more than doubled!

But as I talked with the pastor, he shared an interesting discovery: the new people came in clusters. Out of all that effort and considerable expenditure of money, *80 percent* of the new people were neighbors, friends, people from work, and relatives of those who already attended.

I asked about the posters. Where did they put them? They had the children post them in their *own rooms at home*. Why? Because that's where the children's friends would come. *Children* are the best recruiters of children for the church school.

Out of all that effort, the primary result was to *motivate their own people to share their church with the people closest to them.*

This matches closely the findings of the Institute for American Church Growth, whose questions to over 10,000 lay people indicated that they came into the church in the following ways:[4]

Special Need	2%
Walk-in	3%
Pastor	6%
Visitation	1%
Sunday school	5%
Evangelistic crusade	½%
Program	3%
Friend/relative	79%

Work at learning to share your faith. *You will share it best with those you know the best.*

Sales Techniques

Basic sales techniques can teach us much. A man came to Southern California from Texas. He was a failure there but is a roaring success here at selling cars. His television ads about "Cal Worthington and his dog Spot" are famous; sometimes Spot is an elephant, a leopard, an alligator, a skunk, or even a real dog.

He gets attention in unconventional ways.

Recently he taught a course on sales motivation at an area business seminar. One of the simple things he suggested was "Don't talk too much at the 'close,' or you'll talk yourself right out of the deal."[5]

We need to learn things like that and make them a part of what we do in Kingdom work. How many times do I ask a person to do something, and he says yes? I come back to it a little later, and he says maybe. Suddenly I realize I had better leave it alone, or I'll go away empty-handed.

Again my friend, the encyclopedia salesman, has some basics in techniques that we need to look at. Here are but a few.[6]

First, *the approach*. "Your mental attitude, more than any other single factor" will determine the outcome. "The way you think and feel about your-*self* is telegraphed."

A second point worth sharing: *don't delay*. If you delay calling on friends or relatives because of your fear of taking advantage of them, you may find that when you finally do see them, they have purchased somewhere else.

You may know people who were good friends or neighbors but who joined some other church, and when you asked why, they said, "You never asked me to your church. They did."

Third: "How do you handle an *'unfriendly' person?*" The advice: "You don't." End the effort immediately. Jesus knew all about this. Know when to back off.

Fourth: *speak to the need*. A couple with children just entering school suddenly realizes that their influence will diminish beyond that point. They are often more open to the church. If you can speak to specific needs, you have entrance into their lives.

Finally: the concept of *closure* is important. In every conversation there are several "closes."

The encyclopedia sales manual says, "Concentrate from the very beginning on closing the sale." Be observant and sensitive to the attitudes, emotions, and expressions of the prospect. Frequently, physical actions will signal that it is time for a "close" long before the sales talk calls for it. Watch the body language.

A good "close" tactfully assumes a yes answer. "It is as if you make the decision and the prospect approves."

End the choice question with a downward voice inflection, they suggest, making it a statement rather than a question.

Every closing question should offer the prospect a choice between something and something.

The result of any "close" should be the order or a clear excuse.

In selling, you might say, "You have probably been thinking about buying a program such as this, haven't you?"

Often the person's response, if negative, uncovers questions left unanswered.

It may open the door to your saying, "I understand how you feel" and to begin to share at a deeper level.

Sales theory talks of "audible buying signals." A potential buyer asks: "Do you have a monthly payment plan?" "How much does it cost?" "Is there a savings by paying cash?"

In the church setting: "Do you have a nursery?" "Is there a class for our age group?" "What time do the services start?" When you hear questions such as these, you know the customer is moving toward "buying."

So often we miss the positive responses people are making with their *questions*. We have not worked at it enough to know how to proceed on to a decision.

The salesperson often works out what he wants to say, rehearsing it in front of a mirror, practicing answers to questions that may arise. The encyclopedia salesman suggests that it may take *one hundred visits* before a person feels "at home" with the material and what he is presenting. But the aim is to move beyond the mechanics to a natural, effortless, second-nature approach. And those who do it well do it so effortlessly that in the end you feel he has done *you* a favor by sharing and selling his product!

Our faith must become that way. But on the way to becoming that, as Jesus said, the sons of this world may have much to teach the sons of light (Lk. 16:8) about how we think and react as persons, how life is moved in new directions and energies are invested in new ways.

Paradoxically, the so-called sons of this world sometimes get their clues from the sons of light. A little book entitled *The Greatest Salesman in the*

World[7] outlines the secrets of successful sales and motivation and how one person used them. Who would you guess the author is describing? The apostle Paul.

So the lessons "this world" has distilled from the Scriptures and used for its own ends are surely fair game for the people of God to take back to themselves and put again to use toward their original purpose.

Power for God's Purposes

The *glory* is God's.

And therefore the *power* to make it happen comes from Him, too.

The Spirit helps in at least two ways.

Many scholars refer to *prevenient grace*–a "go-before" grace. Before we ever approach a friend, before we go to some important meeting, before we approach some impossible task, God's Holy Spirit is already there and at work.

If it is God's church, He wants it strong and vital at least as much as we do. And if it is His will that another person have full life, know wholeness, experience meaning and health, is it too much to assume that God is *already at work* in that life, preparing the soil?

How much easier is any task we face when we know that God was there first, already preparing the way.

The second way in which the Spirit works is by *empowering* us. He gives us strength and wisdom beyond our own, gives us words when otherwise we might be speechless (Mk. 13:11), gives us strength when we are by nature fearful.

A simple New Testament faith must be ours: if God wants it done, He will supply the resources.

The Quaker Rufus Jones used to say that if you place a tiny straw parallel to the Gulf Stream, the mighty Gulf Stream will flow through it. If our lives, our dreams, our hopes, our plans are in line with the purposes of God, if our will is in harmony with His will, all the might and power of God Himself will flow through us. And the impossible challenges we

may not even have dared to share with any mortal because they were so grand—those challenges will be accomplished!

Teaching Helps for Chapter 10

Before this class session:

☐ Is there a salesperson in your congregation or among your friends who could come and briefly apply some of the principles of sales to sharing our faith?

☐ Prepare a copy of the Openness Quotient for each student.

☐ Secure the film *Discover Your Gifts,* a powerful film, filled with humor, about a layman struggling to discover what are and what are *not* his gifts.

Suggested Lesson Plan

1. Let each person examine himself and the congregation through use of the Openness Quotient test (Medical Chart 11). Allow three minutes, plus time for grading.

Have them score their own papers as follows:

    5 points for YES to numbers 1, 6, 7, 9, 12.

    10 points for YES to numbers 2, 3, 10, 11, 13, 14, 16, 18, 19, 20.

    15 points for YES on numbers 4, 21, 23.

    Minus 5 for YES on numbers 15 and 17.

    Minus 10 for YES on numbers 5, 8, 22, 25.

    Minus 15 for YES on number 24.

Let them fill in the grading system:

    over 130—excellent

    105 to 125—more than adequate

    100—average

    80 to 95—less than adequate

    under 80—downright difficult to
            break into!

Then discuss the answers. How do you feel about your situation?

2. Silently read Luke 10:1-20. List some of the

"sales" advice in today's language. Are there lessons for us?

Share your lists.

3. *Review* the methods of prospecting listed in Chapter 10. Would any be of value for your congregation? Does your congregation have a prospect list kept up-to-date? If not, name someone to begin working on it.

How will you use it?

4. Show the film *Discover Your Gifts*.

5. Develop ways your congregation could help people become better able to share their faith. Could brief faith-sharing times be a part of responses to church school questions or sharing time in worship?

On the left of a blank piece of paper, have each person list some words or phrases that have become cliches. On the right, translate them into understandable language for an outsider. Allow three minutes. Use the kitchen timer.

Cliches	Translation

Share your findings.

6. Share progress on your individual prospects as well as church assignments.

7. Read together Matthew 23: 1-12. Offer prayers that we all might be less pretentious, more caring, more like Jesus.

1. Donald McGavran, *Understanding Church Growth* (Grand Rapids, Mich.: Eerdmans, 1980), p. 295 ff.

2. Donald McGavran and George G. Hunter III, *Church Growth: Strategies That Work* (Nashville: Abingdon, 1980), p. 108.

3. *Prospecting and Qualifying Your Prospects,* Sales Manual, World Book Encyclopedia, 1981.

4. Charles Arn, Donald McGavran, Win Arn, *Growth: A New Vision for the Sunday School* (Pasadena, Calif.: Church Growth Press, 1980), p. 76. See also footnote on page 90, which indicates that this research has been verified by a research project with the New Orleans Seminary.

5. *Los Angeles Times,* February 4, 1981, part II, p. 2.

6. *Four Steps to the Sale,* Sales Manual, World Book Encyclopedia, 1981.

7. Og Mandino, *The Greatest Salesman in the World* (New York: Bantam, 1968).

Medical Chart 11
Determining Our Openness Quotient

Respond as honestly as possible to the following questions.

Total positive points _____
Total negative points _____
Openness Quotient is _____

_____ Excellent   _____ More than adequate

_____ Average   _____ Less than adequate

	Yes	No	(points plus or minus)
1. Visitors are given ribbons or name tags.			
2. Every worshiper wears a name tag.			
3. Visitors sign a guest book, or there is attendance registration.			
4. There is more than enough parking.			
5. Our sanctuary is full for worship.			
6. Members leave the closest parking spots for the handicapped and visitors.			
7. I take the initiative to talk with those I do not know well.			
8. Our congregation is about the right size.			
9. If someone is sitting alone, I sit by him.			
10. Classrooms are identified.			
11. There is a register of rooms at the entrance.			
12. Rest rooms are easy to find.			
13. Ushers greet people and show them to seats.			
14. Service times and the name of the church are clearly identified outside.			
15. I go to church with a mental list of people I need to see, items I need to check on.			
16. We have a refreshment time following worship.			
17. At fellowship times, I usually spend my time talking with friends.			
18. Visitors to church are visited within 48 hours.			
19. We have some specific strategies for growth.			
20. The church is united on wanting the church to grow.			
21. I feel good about my pastor.			
22. Most of our board members have been members of our congregation for at least five years.			
23. I feel good about our denomination.			
24. There is continual tension in our church.			
25. In the worship service, terms are used and references made that someone new would not understand.			

11 Cathedral Building

On a hill overlooking Venice, Italy, sat a man reported to be the wisest man in the entire area. Two mischievous boys wanted to put him to a test. They approached the old man, one of the boys with his hands cupped, completely hiding whatever was inside.

"Tell us, wise old man," the boy said, "the bird that I hold in my hand, is it alive or is it dead?"

The wise man looked into the boy's eyes and said, "If I tell you it is alive, you will crush it and kill it. If I tell you that it is dead, you will open your hands and set it free. My son," he said, "it shall be as you wish."

You, dear reader, hold the power of life or death for your congregation. Its future is in your hands, and in God's.

Not Overnight

Yet you will not attain your goals all at once. Growing the small church is in some ways like erecting a great Gothic cathedral, which takes generations to build and is, in fact, never finished. Its very lines sweep toward something yet incomplete and forever beyond us.

At the great Washington Cathedral in America's capital, eleven master carvers carefully chiseled the statuary and gargoyles for the magnificent edifice.

One day several years ago, a passerby asked John Fanfani's father, who like his son was one of the artisans on that great cathedral, why he was working so painstakingly on the *back* of a figure. After all, the onlooker pointed out, the back of the figure would never be seen after it was installed.

Fanfani quietly laid aside his mallet and replied, "God will see it."

George Butler, sometimes called the dean of American preachers, used to say to pastors, "Your sermon is your love offering to God. It is not to please the people, the bishop, nor even to please yourself. It is your gift of love to God. And pleasing Him is all that really matters."

We moderns are so programmed to think in terms of what is cost-efficient, practical, and immediate that we have difficulty with the idea of the church being built step by step over a period of years, solidly, to last for generations yet unborn.

With Pain

No great church is built in five years. Never is it built by a people who say, "I quit," at every hard place in the road. Some battles are lost before the war is won. Church building is a long, difficult task, demanding careful attention and our finest skills.

One of Dr. Eden Ryle's motivational films is called *The Pike Syndrome*. A smaller aquarium is suspended inside a larger aquarium. A pike is placed inside the smaller aquarium with minnows swimming about for the pike to feed upon. Then the minnows are removed and placed in the section beyond the pike's reach. The fish lunges for a minnow but bumps its head hard on the glass. Again and again it does this, until finally it realizes that it is only hurting itself. The pike stops trying.

Then the bottom of the smaller aquarium is pulled out. Live food swims all around the pike again. It could have it for the taking. But the fish is so battle-scarred that it has quit trying. It gently moves its fins and sits there . . . and starves!

The lesson is that situations change. God opens new doors. Nothing is ever static. But so often we—who are tired, discouraged, angry, beat—do not change, even when new possibilities lie directly before us.

With Confidence

Dr. Ryle's second film is entitled *You Pack Your Own Chute*. She had never tried skydiving in her life but set out to learn. At one point she asked her instructor, "Aren't you scared your chute won't open?"

His reply was "No, I pack my own chute."

One of the assumptions of Church Growth is that there is no packaged formula for every congregation, no easy gimmick such as busing or following some success pattern from someplace else. Each of us in our own place must grow our own. We must employ the unique talents and personalities of the congregation we serve. We must share who we are in a situation that is unlike any other.

Never downgrade yourself as a part of a small church. Never underestimate the role of your pastor. Having served as pastor of a larger church, I know better when people say, "We could never ask Pastor Frank to serve on that committee or to tackle that task, because he is so terribly busy as pastor of a huge church."

But I know he has secretaries. He has other staff who cover for him in all sorts of ways. He has a minister of visitation (or ministers of visitation). He has janitors to do all kinds of tasks. He may even have a business administrator. He never has to screen incoming phone calls.

No one is busier than the pastor who depends on limited volunteer secretarial help, volunteer janitorial help, who must be part-time youth director, part-time coordinator of programs for the older members, part-time receptionist, and full-time visitation minister. At the same time, of course, he must be a sparkling pulpiteer to match the star who holds forth at grand old First Church and does little more than study and prepare for those few inspiring performances each week.

It takes a lot of talent to pastor a small church. So feel good about your setting. Feel good about your congregation. Feel good about yourself.

A visitor came on some workmen and asked what they were doing. The first said, "I'm earning so much a day."

The second said, "I'm cutting stone."

The third said, "I'm building a cathedral."

You and I, pastors and lay people, are building cathedrals.

The Keys

There are several keys to cathedral building.

First: begin where you are.

After I had been at Glendale several years, a Growth Task Force was formed of several former pastors who were now members in our congregation. We sat in someone's living room and began to think

"No, no, NO—I said over there!"

Reprinted with permission from the Saturday Evening Post Company © 1978

aloud about things we might do.

One man, a former United Presbyterian pastor, said, "It feels like we're trying to be a big church. And we're not. We need to play to our strengths."

Right away I asked him what he meant. How could we do this?

He said, "Well, you have the number present the week before listed in the bulletin of each week. I look down and I see the number 65. Then I look around the sanctuary and see only a handful of people. Up in the choir loft are maybe 15 people. But they're so far away. It would be better if we could take out all the pews and put our chairs in a circle. But short of that, couldn't we get the choir to come down after their anthem and sit with us? We'd have a much better sense of being together and having more people here."

So we tried it. Some of the choir objected at first. Others loved the thought of being able to sit with husband or wife or family.

He went on. "It all seems so formal. We go through the program in the bulletin. I wish we could draw more on the strength of our fellowship in the course of our service."

His suggestion was that I come down and stand between the pews at a point before the offering, invite the sharing of joys and concerns. Maybe we could talk together about our sick members, our successes, the challenges before us.

Announcements had always been difficult for me. In my previous churches I had left them out altogether, expecting people to read the bulletin. But this weekly time of sharing has come to seem very natural, very helpful. Guests are introduced. We feel like a family.

Begin where you are.

Second, affirm who you are. The United Church of Christ study of small churches suggested the need to devise a whole new system to help a church discover its strengths and develop an exciting program . . . if only for 40 people.

As a congregation discovers ministries unique for it, that congregation is given a feeling that it is important.

Third, use your size. Worship centers in a congregation of 600 must be large. They are very difficult. Worship centers in a congregation of 40 can be much simpler to be meaningful.

Sharing joys and concerns in a congregation of 600 is almost impossible.

There are inherent advantages in a small, intimate group. Use them.

Lyle Schaller, in an article for the Disciples of Christ pastors' paper, *Cutting Edge*, lists tips for Church Growth. Among them: *Wear name tags*. Everyone wear name tags. What right do we have to expect new people to memorize all our names while we expect them to make it easy for us by repeatedly telling us their names? No matter how small your congregation, if you have any visitors, provide name tags for everyone.

Add *directional signs*. Make it easy for new people to locate the church and to find their way once there. Don't make coming to church a difficult game that only the most persistent can master.

Also, *fill the pews*. An empty church is discouraging. How do you do this if your sanctuary seats 250 and you have 80 to 100 people present? Schaller says the answer is simple: take out some of the pews! The first to go are usually the back two or three rows. This will open up the back of the nave for an easier flow of traffic. Use the space for literature tables or displays. Or take out some pews up front. Or widen the aisles.

Take away the sense of failure. Help give an impression of vitality.

A Multiple Staff for the Smaller Church

It sounds like a contradiction, doesn't it? But smaller congregations need to build a multiple staff just as large ones do.

As we looked together at spiritual gifts, we talked about "building the skeleton." That skeleton should include some key people very early.

Secretaries–receptionists. Most congregations, however small, have people who are retired or with time on their hands who would willingly be in the church office one morning a week. If they have secretarial skills, they can do secretarial work while there. But even without such skills, they can play a vital role if they bring reading or knitting or letter writing and simply answer the phone or greet visitors. How many valuable opportunities are lost because of an empty office?

Custodians-maintenance workers. Let people volunteer (or enlist them) for one janitorial or yard or maintenance job around the church. A church building that looks unloved does not attract many people.

Undershepherds. But perhaps most important is to enlist persons to share in the work of pastoring. In my first full-time pastorate, I had an elaborate zone or undershepherd plan. The entire congregation was broken into small geographical areas with 8 to 12 family units each. I tried to have each include a variety of active and inactive members. I used color-coded cards: blue (true blue) for active; red for prospectives; yellow for inactives. (At that time there was a toothpaste jingle "You'll wonder where the yellow went. . . .")

We had quarterly meetings of our undershepherds, usually in one of their homes. Each meeting included personal enrichment and training. A physician talked to us about hospital visitation. (He gave simple but helpful instructions such as, "Don't kick the bed. Don't sit on the bed. Don't stay very long. Don't inquire into the nature of the illness.") Some widows shared their early reactions to grief and what kind of ministry by the church would have been most helpful.

Undershepherds served for three years. Terms were staggered. Each year we had a service of dedication during the worship hour. But the system worked only partially. The expectation was that each undershepherd would visit those assigned at least annually, phone or visit in cases of absence, see their people in times of illness or personal crisis, keep me informed of any special needs.

We had report forms, not only for visits but also to share experiences and problems. I even got out a quarterly memo to all the undershepherds, reporting the results and including special quotes that came back to me. I encouraged, pushed, praised, scolded. Some undershepherds worked their areas with great faithfulness. Others never did a thing. The results were spotty at best.

Now in my two smaller congregations, it occurred to me that a variation of this with less expectations could still be helpful. I picked out enough individuals or couples who are active and positive about the church to shepherd about four to eight other units each. They are not asked to visit in homes necessarily, but they are to be aware of which of their four to eight units are or are not in worship, sending a bulletin with a brief note to those absent. If there is a change in attendance pattern, they are to phone the person and to make certain that I am aware of it. They may minister further as they are able.

Other pastoral assistance. In both congregations I have had persons come and offer to help. One man, a college professor, volunteered to give ten hours a week. Earlier he had studied for the Episcopal priesthood. He volunteered to do anything from visiting people to pulling weeds to teaching a class to preaching or assisting in worship. We used him in all of these areas.

The smallest of congregations have retired people with time on their hands. They may get drawn into some kind of community volunteer activity. Or they may sit at home and gradually die. Why not enlist talented, caring, mature people in the service of the church?

I have tried to meet weekly with my college professor volunteer, staying as close to him as I tried to stay with paid staff in my larger congregations.

Small congregations have many resources that can extend the ministries of the church. We need to discover them, enlist them, train and use them, monitoring their efforts as carefully as do the senior pastors of the megachurches.

A former organist at our church in Glendale took a six-week crash course in German at UCLA. She studied every available moment. She crammed with all her ability for the test. She completed the course with an "A."

But two weeks later, she found it difficult to remember a single thing she had learned.

Some churches are built like that.

Cathedrals are not.

Would you believe a congregation can grow too fast? Some growth is cheap growth. Some churches, like toadstools, spring up large and impressive overnight, but they are soft and mushy. I can show you some giants that came on like gang busters but faded once they were exposed to the burning light of day.

Dean Kelley, mentioned earlier as the author of *Why Conservative Churches Are Growing,* is interviewed in the film *How to Grow a Church.* When asked about his own denomination, he says in part that too many members were brought in too quickly, too easily, without understanding or sufficient commitment. He mentions having lectured on this very problem at a Unitarian church. At the end of his lecture, the pastor announced that anyone who wanted to become a member of that congregation should simply sign the membership book at the back! That, said Kelley, was the very kind of thing he was objecting to.

Across many pop bottles these days is a line we need to understand: "No deposit—no return." If a person invests nothing, there will be no strong ties to keep him. Easy come, easy go.

An inquirer's class is a way of leading people into serious membership. Whenever I have three or four new people in church, I begin a class that runs for five weeks during the church school hour. When people have been at church a few weeks, I visit them in their homes and invite them, telling them the class is a way to learn more about the church, but it does not obligate them to join. With a core of a few, I announce the starting time several weeks ahead, publicly inviting others who might be interested.

In larger churches, I have held these classes almost continuously. It has been my experience that after five weeks together, it is easy to visit people in their homes and invite them to become members. Few say no, because they have had time to think about it. It focuses their thoughts toward a decision. They have a firmer basis for joining. It does not seem hasty to them. To attend too long without such an experience allows people to settle into a pattern of being onlookers, not full members.

As you build, *build well*. Be sure people know the directions of your belief. Give them an experience rooted in Biblical faith. Make certain they have a clear understanding of the contract.

Jesus did not make it easy. "If any man will come after me, let him deny himself, and take up his cross, and follow me" (Mt. 16:24).

The paradox of growth is that those who seek it as an end in itself often end up with very little. Those who set out to be strong, faithful churches often find growth coming despite themselves. *Strong churches grow.* Those that try to be everything to everybody often end up being very little to anybody.

The Impossible Dream

A select group of 133 lay leaders and clergy of the United Methodist Church has indicated they do not feel their denomination will grow in the years ahead.[2] They forecast consolidation, not growth, in the next two decades.

They see a threat to church-owned property, in-creased costs and smaller enrollments in its related colleges and institutions, a decline in all areas of membership and participation—worship, church school, and every other area of active church involvement. "The church will lack the will or resolve to take the steps necessary to prepare itself to be what it hopes to be." It will administer its past or simply describe its present symptoms. It will not be a dynamic force in a rapidly changing world.

If all United Methodists shared that assumption, it would surely become a self-fulfilling prophecy. Fortunately, all do not.

When George Hunter, who heads the United Methodist staff for evangelism, assumed his job, he took his staff to Fuller Theological Seminary's School of World Mission for training in the principles of Church Growth. His intentions are that his church will turn outward.

Hunter insists that all trends indicate that the direction toward loss will bottom out by the fall of 1983. He calls it "a noble experiment. No denomination in our culture has ever shown such sustained decline and then turned it around."

Asked about his own psychological health in the face of such odds, he replies with a twinkle in his eyes, "I sleep like a baby. I sleep two hours . . . wake up and cry two hours . . . then sleep some more."

If the turnaround comes, he insists, the Church Growth as a movement and its literature will be the cause more than anything else. It is giving their 39,000 congregations "legs to stand on" and "eyes to see their apostolic task."

The change has already begun, he insists. In the areas where they have focused—in every target population—the turnaround has already come.

God has a dream for His people. It is not sickness and death, inactivity and decline. It is new life, vigor, hope, new and clearer ministries for Him.

Jack Hayford, who took the small, struggling First Foursquare Church of Van Nuys, was terribly discouraged in his first months there. But he committed his life to God and pledged his willingness to be pastor of a small church the rest of his life, if that was what God wanted.

A few days later, according to Pastor Jack, God got back to him and said, "I have other plans for you and this church. I have dreams you wouldn't even believe if they were all spelled out. I will use you mightily in this place." The subsequent story of The Church on the Way is well-known.

All things excellent are as difficult as they are rare.

Rome was not built in a day. Neither was your church building. Nor the congregation that God intends for you in your place.

They all take time, dogged persistence, and huge handfuls of patience, which God will give to us as we open life to Him. And with the gift of patience follow other countless riches that can come only as *that* gift unlocks the door.

Teaching Helps for Chapter 11

Before the class session:

☐ Talk with your congregational leaders (or pastor) about a Growth Task Force, how it might best be formed, to whom it should relate. Discuss also the feasibility of a Church Growth dinner. Explore some possible dates.

Think together about projections for growth. What is realistic? Make it high enough to challenge but not so high as to discourage. Normal biological growth should result in a 5-percent membership increase per year.

☐ Secure the film *But I'm Just a Layman*, a moving story of a layman's struggle to see that the work of the Great Commission does not belong to the pastor alone. Filled with humor.

☐ Prepare copies of Medical Chart 12 for everyone.

Suggested Lesson Plan

1. Review the progress, failures, and successes in winning your own prospect to Christ.

Review the progress in the congregation toward a growth awareness.

2. Discuss: "Are we trying to be a big church?"

Individually, list some ways you could maximize your strengths as a small church. Allow three minutes. Use the kitchen timer.

Then share your lists. List items on a chalkboard. Are some worth pursuing?

3. Discuss cheap growth. "Are we building solidly and well? Are there classes for all who come into the church?"

4. Look at the charts you developed for your congregation in chapter 3. What would be a realistic expectation for growth in the next ten years? Chart it together on Medical Chart 12. Can the entire congregation consider and adopt such a goal? What specific steps are necessary to meet such a goal?

What gifted persons (retired, underemployed, or volunteers) are available for work in your church? What jobs would you like to see accomplished? What do the available people see that needs doing? Explore the possibility of a Parish Volunteer Service or a job match to talent.

Recount God's persistence with people: Abraham's promise of a son, Moses' 40 years in the wilderness to build a nation, the Babylonian Captivity of 70 years, the 400 years of waiting for the Messiah.

Cathedral building involves an architect's plan, an estimate of cost of materials and workmanship, and a labor force to see the plan to completion (all of which the church is made aware and is allowed to vote on). Does your church have an overall plan of action for growth of which everyone is aware—and allowed to give input? A budget? A core of workers? Materials?

5. Organize a Growth Task Force. It may come from volunteers out of this study group. They need to meet at least monthly, review progress, suggest ways the church can organize for growth. They should be responsible to the church board. Such a group is essential to growth.

6. Consider a Church Growth Banquet (similar to an Every-Member Canvass Loyalty Dinner). Use a few short speeches, with overhead transparencies. Present the facts and the challenge. At the close, give each person a card on which they can commit themselves in this area.

7. *Read together* Acts 1:6-8. Offer your prayers for your church.

Following the Church Growth Banquet, plan for at least quarterly all-church meetings on growth. The first might well focus on the church school. Recruit as many teachers, youth, and adult class officers as possible to be present. Use the excellent film The Great Commission Sunday School.

Plan to keep the emphasis before your congregation.

The important thing is that you develop a program tailored for your needs, tooled to your own strengths.

God's richest blessing as you embark on this rewarding new adventure for Him!

1. Lyle E. Schaller, ''Twelve Tips for Church Growth,'' *Cutting Edge* (Vol. 8, No. 5, September-October 1979), p. 1 ff.
2. Alan K. Waltz, *Images of the Future* (Nashville: Abingdon, 1980), reports on the projections of a ''Delphi panel'' of 133 clergy and lay persons regarding the next two decades of the United Methodist Church. See also ''Next 20 years troubled ones for Church: Panel,'' *Open Circuit,* the United Methodist Publishing House employee newspaper, October 1980, p. 1.

LET'S GROW
Commitment Card

Believing it is God's will that our church grow, I hereby commit myself to actively seek to involve _____ new person(s) in our church fellowship during the coming year.

Signed _____

Medical Chart 12
Ten-year projected growth for
our church school
our worship
our communicant resident membership

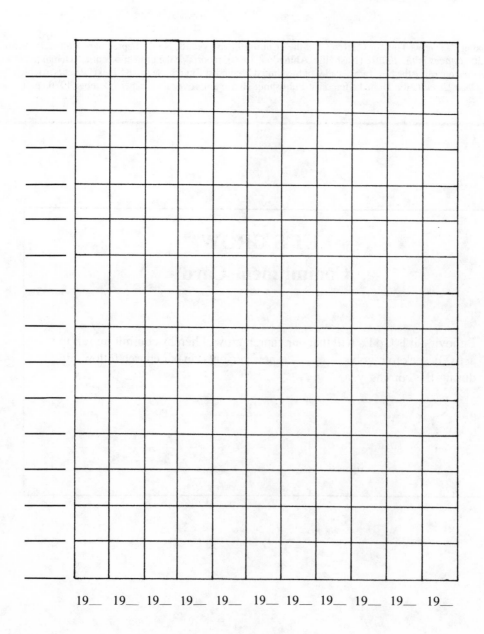

19__ 19__ 19__ 19__ 19__ 19__ 19__ 19__ 19__ 19__ 19__

Resources

Win Arn, Donald McGavran, and Charles Arn, *Growth: A New Vision for the Sunday School* (Pasadena, Calif.: Church Growth Press, 1980).

Floyd Bartel, *A New Look at Church Growth* (Scottdale, Pa.: Mennonite Publishing House, 1979).

Jackson W. Carroll, ed., *Small Churches Are Beautiful* (New York: Harper and Row, 1977).

Carl S. Dudley, *Making the Small Church Effective* (Nashville: Abingdon, 1978).

Dean R. Hoge and David A. Roozen, eds., *Understanding Church Growth and Decline, 1950-1978* (New York: Pilgrim, 1979).

Dean M. Kelley, *Why Conservative Churches Are Growing* (New York: Harper and Row, 1972).

W. Curry Mavis, *Advancing the Smaller Church* (Grand Rapids, Mich.: Baker, 1968).

Donald A. McGavran, *Understanding Church Growth,* fully revised (Grand Rapids, Mich.: Eerdmans, 1980).

Donald A. McGavran and Winfield C. Arn, *Ten Steps for Church Growth* (New York: Harper and Row, 1977).

Donald McGavran and George G. Hunter III, *Church Growth: Strategies That Work* (Nashville: Abingdon, 1980).

Lyle E. Schaller, *Assimilating New Members* (Nashville: Abingdon, 1978).

Lyle E. Schaller, *The Change Agent* (Nashville: Abingdon, 1978).

Lyle E. Schaller, *Effective Church Planning* (Nashville: Abingdon, 1979).

Lyle E. Schaller, *Hey, That's Our Church* (Nashville: Abingdon, 1975).

Lyle E. Schaller, *Survival Tactics in the Parish* (Nashville: Abingdon, 1977).

Robert H. Schuller, *Your Church Has Real Possibilities* (Glendale, Calif.: Regal, 1974).

C. Peter Wagner, *Your Church Can Be Healthy* (Nashville: Abingdon, 1979).

C. Peter Wagner, *Your Church Can Grow* (Glendale, Calif.: Regal, 1976).

C. Peter Wagner, *Your Spiritual Gifts Can Help Your Church Grow* (Glendale, Calif.: Regal, 1979)

Wayne Zunkel and Irven Stern, *Invitation to Adventure: a twelve-week study/action course on church growth;* student workbook and color overheads (Elgin, Ill.: Brethren Press, 1979).

Some studies of small churches include:

David J. Brown, Robert Haskins, and William Swisher, *Small Church Project* (New York: United Church Board for Homeland Ministries, 1977).

David J. Brown, *Washington Small Church Project* (Wenatchee, Wash.: United Ministries, 1976).

Theodore H. Erickson, *Small by Design* (Lancaster, Pa.: Lancaster Theological Seminary, 1977).

Local Church Development II (Wenatchee, Wash.: United Ministries, 1979).

Some important agencies:
L.E.A.D. Consultants, Inc.
P.O. Box 311
Pittsford, NY 14534

Institute for American Church Growth
709 E. Colorado Blvd., #150
Pasadena, CA 91101 (213) 449-4400
24 hours toll-free 800-423-4844

Fuller Theological Seminary, for courses in Church Growth
135 N. Oakland Ave.
Pasadena, CA 91101 (213) 449-1745

Department of Church Growth
Charles E. Fuller Institute of Evangelism and Church Growth
P.O. Box 989
Pasadena, CA 91102 (213) 449-0425

8   1290

Zunkel, Wayne C.
AUTHOR
Growing the Small Church
TITLE
Passing on the Promise Resource